The Popcorn Principle

The Popcorn Principle

7 Significant Truths to Stay at the Top

Jerry LePre

Joyful Life Publishing

Library of Congress Cataloging-in-Publication Data

LePre, Christopher Gerard "Jerry," 1955-
    The Popcorn Principle : 7 Significant truths to stay at the top /
Jerry LePre, LLC
        p. cm.
    Includes bibliographical references.

ISBN: 9798366546065

    1. Business and Economics: Workplace Culture
    2. Business and Economics: Organizational Development

Printed in the United States of America
Joyful Life Publishing
Destrehan, LA 70047

Smell The Popcorn™, Popcorn Person™, Pop to the Top™, Stay at the Top™, and Popcorn Person Logo are trademarks of Christopher Gerard LePre.

This book is dedicated to Gen. Richard I. Neal, USMC (ret). Gen. Neal was a great man, leader, and mentor. His life impacted so many. His legacy will not be forgotten. Thank you for turning this drummer boy into a man. His wisdom continues to inspire me today.
Rest in peace.

A.M.D.G.
Ad majorem Dei gloriam
For the greater glory of God

Foreword by
Ryan C. Lowe

A basic goal common to all of us is the desire to achieve the significance of success. This is our purpose and our quest to change the world by making a difference.

However, despite this wish, many people allow circumstances to dictate their life-paths. Their submission creates a legacy of mediocrity that restricts them from reaching their true potential. As a result, these people lose focus of their purpose while succumbing to setbacks, challenges, and fears.

Let me ask you this, if someone offered you a blueprint to discover the value of your life, "How much would that information be worth to you?"

Although it is impossible to put a dollar amount on this type of advice, you will agree that life-changing insight like this would be priceless.

Yet I can tell you that Jerry LePre's book *The Popcorn Principle: 7 Significant Truths to Stay at the Top* provides priceless information that makes a difference in your life so you can make a difference with your life.

Without a doubt, when you invest the time to read and follow the wisdom in *The Popcorn Principle*, Jerry's powerful and engaging truths will empower you to grow to your full potential and achieve the significance of greatness.

During my career as a professional speaker, author, and trainer, I have found that books with the magnitude of *The Popcorn Principle* are the ones that inspired me to go far beyond my dreams and levels of success.

While Jerry's first book, *Smell The Popcorn: 12 Life-changing Secrets to Pop to the Top*, gave you the tools to reach the top, this book motivates you to stay there by thinking forward.

When I met Jerry at a National Speakers Association meeting in New Orleans, I knew he was a man of integrity and vision with a purpose and a passion for helping others. I loved his positive attitude and his selfless spirit. It was refreshing to meet an author and speaker who practices what he preaches. His highly effective mentoring is making a huge difference in the lives of countless people by helping them *Pop to the Top* and *Stay at the Top*.

I personally challenge you to read *The Popcorn Principle* from cover to cover and, as you read it, grab a pen and paper so you can take lots of notes. Focus especially on the areas of your life where change needs to take place.

Don't wait. Start today. It's time you take responsibility for your life. No excuses! I know that by implementing the wisdom of Jerry's *The Popcorn Principle*, it will transform you from a being an indifferent faker into a thriving difference maker.

Ryan C. Lowe
Speaker and Author of
Get off Your Attitude, Change Your Attitude, Change Your Life

Testimonials

"I thought that Jerry's *Smell the Popcorn* was the perfect snack to perk me up in rough times, but he has exceeded my expectations with *The Popcorn Principle*. This book made me hungry for the smell of continued success and to keep striving to be a Purpose Driven Person."

Bruce S. Wilkinson, CSP
Speaker and Author of *The Thermostat Leader*

"Jerry is a passionate and knowledgeable leader. His unique approach to training and development reflects the one of a kind insight he brings to others. Jerry has put years of research in his models and I continue to be impressed."

Julie Couret
New Orleans #1 Executive Coach

"Jerry LePre has provided a valuable service for this fast-paced world. In easy-to-read language, his book (*The Popcorn Principle*) is something one can pick up, open to any page, and find inspiration and encouragement."

Carol Allen, PhD
Author of *Leah Chase: Listen, I Say Like This*

"Like a kernel of corn,
you may have to lose who you are to find
who you are meant to be."

Table of CONTENTS

"When faced with the heat of adversity,
champions are forged by the fire while the
others are consumed by its flames."

- Jerry LePre
The Popcorn Destiny

Introduction

The path was long, and the climb was rough,
but the view from the top is well worth it.

Stay at the Top

So you reached the top. What's next? Where do you go from here?

Those are the questions that most people who have *popped to the top* and achieved success have repeatedly asked themselves. What do I do now?

In working with people both professionally and personally, I found most successful people, people of significance, still thirst for the next adventure. These accomplished *Difference Makers* aren't satisfied to just sit back and mildew in a rocking chair.

They live for the new success story.

They live for the journey.

They live for the passion of discovery.

My book, *Smell The Popcorn: 12 Life-changing Secrets to Pop to the Top*, empowered its readers to grow from the heat of adversity and achieve significance. Yet significance isn't static. The 'top' is not a fixed point. It's alive and still popping to greater heights. *(See Appendix A on page 119.)*

The entrepreneurial spirit that took these *Difference Makers* to the 'top' isn't dead. Their appetite to sustain significance is alive. It's a constant hunger to passionately seek new and exciting quests that drives these visionaries.

However, they don't have to look too far to find the quests they seek. Staying at the 'top' is their next great journey, since staying there is often more challenging than getting there.

To maintain their position at the 'top' takes a fresh forward-thinking vision. After all, the success *Difference Makers* experience today serves only as a standard for raising the bar (top) for future success.

Most people who reach the top are masters of thinking forward. Unfortunately not all are *Forward Thinkers*. Those who are not, will find it difficult or even impossible to *Stay at the Top*™.

Forward Thinkers constantly take their journey to a higher level. They realize the scenery (view) gets better the higher they climb.

My book, *The Popcorn Principle (Book 2 of the Pop to the Top Series)*, builds on the wisdom of *Smell the Popcorn* (Book 1). It's *Seven Significant Truths* engage and energize forward-thinking climbers to keep popping to new heights.

"Smell The Popcorn" Summary Review

"When you are saddened by the heat of trouble, do you act like a kernel of corn or a chocolate candy bar?"

This was the question my Sunday school teacher asked her class many years ago.

Before you give your answer, you need to know that a kernel of corn changes into popcorn when faced with tremendous heat while a candy bar melts into a gooey mess.[1]

Now that you understand the difference, which one do you want to be like - the thing that explodes into something great to eat or the thing that softens into a messy glob?

Our response to the heat of adversity determines if we climb to the top or stagnate in the mess of mediocrity. In other words, do we choose the greatness and significance of our purpose, or do we settle for less?

The forward-thinking popcorn mentality, which is rooted in your V.A.L.U.E. Core, chooses significance every time.

The acronym stands for *Vision, Attitude, Love, Understanding,* and *Energy* with the greatest being love. Without passion (love) to guide us to the vision, the significance of success is never found. Any victory that lacks love is shallow and meaningless. *(See Appendix B on page 121.)*

Smell The Popcorn Metaphor

Be it at a movie theater, a sporting event, or home, when I smell popcorn, I know a special treat is ready to be enjoyed. In the same way, when the seeds of our potential, like kernels of corn, are transformed by the heat of adversity to *Pop to the Top*™, we metaphorically *Smell The Popcorn*™ of our success.

Are you a Popcorn Person? (*See Appendix C on page 123.*)

Definition of The Popcorn Principle

Unlike years ago when I was a child, families now enjoy delicious popcorn at home in a matter of minutes and without the mess. This modern convenience was made possible by the creation of microwave popcorn. No longer do we need to heat oil in a pan on the stove before pouring in the kernels, putting the lid on, and sliding the pan from side to side over the flame.

Nowadays all we do is follow the instructions on the packaging. As long we adhere to the step-by-step directions, the popcorn will be great every time.

This process is an example of *The Popcorn Principle*[2] which states when specific actions are repeated consistently in the proper sequences, the desired result will be the same every time. Even small actions (habits) done consistently, can produce extraordinary results.

However, the slightest deviation in the process will yield an undesired outcome. Sometimes this deviation is caused by external forces and in some cases, it's due to operator error or lack of judgement. After all, when you stop the microwave earlier or longer than directed, the popcorn is not perfect. Success is the same way.

Yet when *Seven Significant Truths* (habits) are applied to *The Popcorn Principle,* this rule no longer confines *Forward Thinkers* to the current follow-the-directions methods. Instead, innovators are empowered to use today's methods as a platform to launch tomorrow's innovations.

Forward Thinkers Invest in the Future

Forward Thinkers are trailblazing pioneers invested in the future. Their purpose is inspired by the past, rooted in today, and driven by their passion for tomorrow.

Their purpose is inspired by the past, rooted in today, and driven by their passion for tomorrow.

Forward thinking methods generate a futuristic outlook that harnesses the power of the moment with imagination, critical thinking, and practical wisdom. A realistic vision of the next generation of innovations and opportunities is created by this thought process.[3]

Forward Thinkers foresee the best path for attaining and maintaining significance by defining and aligning expectations for the mission with available resources. Thus, these visionaries are empowered to anticipate and respond to future challenges by designing a flexible framework to overcome them.[4]

When grounded with core values[5], *Forward Thinkers* invest in the future without sacrificing the present or ignoring the past. These value-based visionaries combine the strength of integrity with the power of innovation. Their guidance inspires and encourages forward thinking and creativity in others who share the journey to the top and above.

In addition to empowering *Forward Thinkers* who have reached the top *Stay at the Top*™, the *Seven Significant Truths* along with the *12 Life-changing Secrets* provide the tools for those beginning their journey to *Smell the Popcorn.*

Seven Significant (Transformative) Truths to Stay at the Top
1. Rise and Shine
2. Think B.I.G.! Think W.O.W.!
3. Take the Path Less Traveled
4. Strike Up the Band (Organic Approach to DEI)
5. Make a Difference; Not Excuses
6. Avoid the *Ain't Dere No More* Syndrome
7. Sing Your Own Song

Success is a journey, not a destination.

-Ben Sweetland

Rise and Shine

"Stop complaining and do something...
Shut up! Rise up! Grow up! And Show up!
See you at the Top."

- Israelmore Ayvivor

1

Rise and Shine / Conquer the Day

We must first find the truth in yesterday
before we can live the truth today.
Only then will we possess the wisdom
to discover the truth for tomorrow.

Every day we rise and shine to a new day. Every day is a new beginning. Every day is filled with opportunities to make a difference. Every day we have a choice to follow our purpose or be stuck in our past. *Forward Thinkers* <u>rise</u> and <u>shine</u> to the occasion.

No matter the problems we faced yesterday, the fact is they were yesterday's problems. They are not today's, unless we make them. *Forward Thinkers* don't make them. They rise above them.

Forward Thinkers know new beginnings start each day with a fresh and positive perspective to life. Today we are empowered to respond with a renewed commitment to rise above our troubles and shine like never before.

You don't need a camera to capture the moment, nor do you need physical strength to conquer the day. All you need is an open mind to unleash the power of possibilities.

As I said in *Smell The Popcorn* (Secret #2), this is the time to *Renew Your Mind. (See Appendix D on page 125.)* It begins with meditation.

For an effective *Forward Thinker* each day begins in a quiet place with an untainted mindset. This sets the tone for the day.

Our daily renewal instills the mental discipline, confidence, and persistence to persevere in tough times and empowers new growth to think forward. Life is all about growing. It's about change.

Afterall, it doesn't matter if the glass is half-full or half-empty. What matters is what's inside of it. This is your time to refill your glass of life with the positive significance to rise and shine. It's also the moment to shatter any glass still filled with negativity that may be buried in the dark places of your mind. Shatter this old glass, before it shatters your life.

Unlike Eastern Cultures where the emphasis of meditation is on the state of emptiness, a *Forward Thinker's* mindset meditates on the fullness of life. This self-awareness reflects on the wisdom, creativity, harmony, and beauty of life found in the past, present, and envisioned for the future.

The rise and shine mental states of self-awareness are:

- **Silence**

  Avoid all distractions for total concentration.

- **Solitude**

  Focus on one-on-one connection with creation.

- **Serenity**

  Release negative energy to obtain inner peace and joy.

- **Solace**

  Discover the comfort in who you are and who you can be.

- **Submission**

  Rebuke ego; surrender to the harmony of humility.

Building the Framework for Tomorrow

The way we think and act today to inspire success cannot always be focused on the same thoughts that started us on our roads to success. Neither can it be the mindset that sustains the future vision.

Today's mentality can only serve as framework for the vision of tomorrow. A framework built on a foundation of wisdom from life lessons learned in the past.

"Progress is impossible without change, and those who cannot change their minds cannot change anything," George Bernard Shaw said.

Change does not come from without; it comes from within.

As I said earlier, once you *Pop to the Top*™, it takes as much, if not more, energy to *Stay at the Top*™ since the perspective of the top is always rising. The world is changing, and so must we if we expect to rise to new heights.

Change starts with a decision. It starts with you. It starts in your mind. Change does not come from without; it comes from within.

The Sixth Truth, *Avoid the Ain't Dere No More Syndrome*, provides learning examples of iconic organizations who made wrong decisions for change regarding growth and perpetuation. As a result, they *Ain't Dere No More.*[1] An example of a positive forward-thinking decision to change is also given in this chapter.

Rise Up After the Fall

"The greatest accomplishment is not in never falling, but in rising again after you fall," Vince Lombardi said.

For those of us who grew up in the Greater New Orleans (GNO) area, we can count on the fact that the Mississippi River will rise again. But we can also count on the fact that when faced with adversity, the people from this area will always rise to the occasion.

To us, life is all about faith, family, football, and food.

We know how to laugh.

We know how to love.

We know how to cry.

To sum it up, we know how to live.

And more importantly, we know when something threatens who we are, we will show them who we are.

No matter what we face. No matter how bad it gets.

Be it from nature or manmade.

We won't give up. We won't surrender.

We will always rebuild bigger, better, and stronger.

Together, we will rise above the waterline.

Together, we will shine brighter than ever.

Like the NOLA risers, our journey to discover significance is full of obstacles, setbacks, and crisis situations. The journey can be rough and long. Even the best of us will get knocked down. Yet the best of us don't stay down. Be like the best. Rise up after the fall!

"Getting knocked down in life is a given. Getting up and moving forward is a choice," Zig Ziglar said.

Key Roles and Traits to Shine

When you see things differently, you make a difference. You change the world. You shine.

Throughout history, civilization has benefited from *Forward Thinkers* who shined.

Leonardo Da Vinci, Isaac Newton, Stephen Hawking, Albert Einstein[2], Galileo Galilei, and the Greek philosophers Aristotle, Socrates, and Plato are a few of the great futuristic minds that changed the history of the world.

Closer to home, America has its own group of shining *Forward Thinkers*, such as Thomas Edison, Sarah E. Goode[3], and Nikola Tesla[4]. They are a small sampling of our country's brilliant minds.

However, America's greatest example of forward thinking is the "Constitution" of the United States. It's a living document since the spirit of its words are applicable to current issues.[5]

Our founding fathers who wrote the "Constitution" were *Forward Thinkers*. These patriots crafted a living document that remains the foundation for the spirit of law for our country almost 250 years later.

Despite being separated by centuries, miles, language, and cultures, these *Forward Thinkers* shared commonalities (talent and abilities) that made them stand out from the crowd.

For some the following list of skills[6] came naturally while others worked to develop them through experiencing life. No matter how acquired, *Forward Thinkers* use their talents to shine.

Futurist / Visionary

The ability to harmonize creativity with analytical critical thinking is the primary role needed for *Forward Thinkers* to shine. They think BIG. (Second Truth)

This thought process identifies future opportunities, challenges, and trends along with determining the intellectual talent, financial contributors, and available resources to ensure a high level of success. To these innovators the vision of the future isn't only possible; they believe it's probable.

Gatherer

Forward Thinkers bring together the right people (talent and contributors), at the right time, for the right reason with the right resources. Without one of these ingredients, the journey may not get started and if it does, it won't last. Even with the right people, if the resources or contributions are not available, the path to success won't shine for long. Gathering is discussed in the Fourth Truth.

Also, timing is critical. It's not wise to start a seafood restaurant if the supply chain is disrupted. You don't want to advertise fresh fish; when you can't get fresh fish.

Influential Communicator

Defining and effectively communicating the vision, goals, and mission(s) without compromising core values is a must for *Forward Thinkers*. These dynamic communicators use empathy to engage and influence their team to buy into the process. Clarifying the specific goals and missions for individuals and groups is critical to establish expectations, responsibilities, and accountability. (*See page 80.*)

Consider the sales and accounting teams have different goals, roles, and missions but no matter their unique function, both share the same unified vision and core values. Forward-thinking communicators shine when they relate to all groups with empathic guidance. (*See page 69.*)

Adaptor (Adaptable / Fluid Motion)

Forward Thinkers are prepared intellectually and emotionally to adapt to future trends and challenges. As stated in *Smell The Popcorn*, these visionaries identify potential trials with mitigation methods (*prolutions*), which is short for proactive solutions.

Yet despite in-depth research and planning, unanticipated trials will happen. In 2020, Covid was an unexpected challenge that changed the world. Other factors that impact the vision of the future include inflation, catastrophic natural disasters, social changes, and politics.

Forward Thinkers are flexible. Thus they eagerly make the necessary changes to the fluid motion of the mission without distorting the core vision and values.

Trooper (Persevere)

Forward Thinkers who exhibit extreme perseverance, fortitude, and tenacity are called troopers. They don't get discouraged, even when results aren't happening right away or as expected.

These *Difference Makers* know greatness doesn't happen overnight and it's not always a smooth road. It takes grit. It takes sacrifices. It takes perseverance to shine.

Like making popcorn, to get the best results, you must wait for the right amount of time. Troopers don't force the issue.

Initiator (Source of Accountability)

Forward-thinking and effective leaders define and initiate the culture of accountability. It begins with them being accountable for their own words, actions, and behavior, as well as for those that follow them. When things go wrong, *Forward Thinkers* accept the blame and consequences. Instead of excuses, they foresee solutions with corrective actions.

Forward Thinkers, who step out from the crowd of managers, don't point fingers; they point teams in the right direction.

The Fifth Truth discusses steps to plant and cultivate such a culture.

"When a man (person) points a finger at someone else, he (she or they) should remember that four of his (her or their) fingers are pointing at himself (herself or themselves)," Louis Nizer said.

A Light in Darkness

The tiny lighthouse stood alone on the shore,
After years of service it was needed no more.
Its light, its love, no longer shined,
Replaced with technology by people who were blind.
Blind to the fact that the lighthouse was more than brick and stone,
It was a faithful loving friend who guided lost travelers home.

Like a lighthouse, *Forward Thinkers* can be a beacon of light to those who are in the dark about finding their purpose. When we shine to help others, we make a difference. Our light serves as a guide to lead and empower others who are searching for hope for today and significance for tomorrow.

Significant *Forward Thinkers* don't neglect or abandon the past (the old lighthouse); they build on it and perfect it. They shine on the path less taken (Third Truth) to guide travelers home to the vision.

Your Moment to Rise and Shine

A *Popcorn Moment* is the wakeup call to rise to the occasion and shine for today and tomorrow. It's the pivotal times in our lives that offer another chance for us to make a significant difference.

When the heat of adversity is at its hottest, a *Popcorn Moment* for significance is the brightest. But no matter how hot things get, this is the moment to shine. Make your *Popcorn Moment* a *Significant Moment*.

Go to Bat for Change[7]

"A life is not important except in the impact it has on other lives," Jackie Robinson said.

When the time came for Jackie Robinson to go to bat, he rose and shined to the occasion. He discovered his *Popcorn Destiny*. *(See page 12)*

In April of 1947, Robinson became the first African American baseball player to start at game in modern day Major League Baseball (MLB). Robinson, who played for the Brooklyn Dodgers, was inducted in the Baseball Hall of Fame in 1962.

During his illustrious 10-year MLB career, Robinson was a six time all-star. In addition to winning *Rookie of the Year* honors, the star first baseman was the first black player to win the *National League Most Valuable Player* Award in 1949.

To honor his legacy, his uniform number "42" was retired by all major league teams in 1997. He was the first professional athlete in any sport to be so honored.

In 2004, MLB adopted the annual tradition of celebrating *Jackie Robinson Day*. On this day of celebration, every MLB player on every team wears the number "42" in his honor.

When given his chance by a forward-thinking baseball executive, Jackie Robinson made a difference. He made an impact.

When faced with your *Popcorn Moment*, go to bat. This is your time to rise and shine and achieve your *Popcorn Destiny*.

Rise & Shine

Every moment is a fresh beginning.

-T.S. Elliot

Think B.I.G.!
Think W.O.W.!

Bold & Innovative Goals create

Wonderful Opportunities for Winning

"Creative people must entertain lots of silly ideas in order to receive the occasional strokes of genius."

- Marshall J. Cook

2

Don't Magnify the Problem

When it comes to facing a problem of any type, we often make the challenge, setback, or bad news appear bigger than it is. I must confess. I sometimes use a magnifying glass when I look at things that don't go as planned. Do you?

The first critical step when facing a problem is to throw away the magnifying glass. Start seeing the problem as it really is and not what we made it to be. Reframe the situation to see the positive. Process sadness and then dream about the possibilities.

When we look with a clear vision at what appears to be a negative situation, we see the solution. In fact, when we see our problems as they really are, we see how big we really are at defeating them.

Think **B.I.G.!**

BOLD INNOVATIVE GOALS

Think **W.O.W.!**

WONDERFUL OPPORTUNITIES for WINNING

How Significant is BIG?

There are so many ways to describe BIG. When it comes to height, a big person is considered tall. When it comes to weight, a big person is referred to as obese. At Starbucks a big coffee is called *Venti*. At a typical department store a big size shirt for men has a tag showing 4X.

The fact is BIG has lots of names. Think about it. What determines big?

A 6'2" male is considered tall for the average person. Yet if he plays basketball in the NBA, he is short. Speaking of the NBA, when 7'1" Tyson Chandler, the former center for the New Orleans Hornets, stood next to 7'6" Yao Ming, formerly of the Rockets, Chandler looked short. However, when Chandler stood next to future NBA hall-of-fame point guard and former teammate Chris Paul (CP3), Paul looked very short even though he is almost 6'0" tall.

Everything considered, size is relative since it is based on comparison. Although size doesn't matter, significance does.

Author Mary O'Conner said, "It is not how busy you are, but why you are busy. The bee is praised. The mosquito swatted."

The difference is the significance of their work. The bee pollinates flowers. The mosquito annoys.

The fact size is irrelevant is especially true for describing a person who is a BIG thinker with BIG goals. It doesn't matter if you are short or tall, skinny or fat. What matters most is the size of your W.O.W. Factor, which is measured by the size of your spirit, your heart, your determination, and your imagination. This is how *Forward Thinkers* gauge significance.

It doesn't matter who you are or where you come from. You can be rich, or you can be poor. It costs nothing to think B.I.G. and think W.O.W. Yet the results are priceless.

Everyone can be a BIG thinker. Everyone can think WOW. When you think like that, nothing can stop you.

In Ray Bradbury's science fiction short story *A Sound of Thunder*, a group of hunters go back in time to kill dinosaurs. However, on one prehistoric safari, a butterfly is accidently killed. As a result of this butterfly's death, all history is changed. This forms part of the genealogy of the term Butterfly Effect.[1]

If the life of a tiny butterfly, which seems so insignificant, can make such a powerful difference that changes the world as we know it, how much more of a difference can you make with your life?

Thinking B.I.G. has no limitations when you add the W.O.W. Factor. Once you light the fire of your imagination, the flames of success are ignited.

Like the butterfly, you can become a significant *Difference Maker*. You can *Pop to the Top*™ and *Stay at the Top*™.

Be <u>Bold</u>, Be <u>Innovative</u>, Be <u>Positive</u>

Like him or not, former United States president and billionaire real estate tycoon Donald Trump spoke these impactful words:

"As long as you're going to be thinking anyway, think big."

Experts say our thoughts make us who we are. So why not think bold and think innovative thoughts. In other words, think B.I.G.! Think W.O.W.! Think POSITIVE!

Dr. Norman Vincent Peale, author of *The Power of Positive Thinking*, believed thoughts shape a person's destiny. He said negative thoughts filled with hate and defeat result in failure while sincere, dynamic, and positive thoughts of love, service, and success destine a person to future greatness. *(See Appendix D Tactics to Renew Your Mind on page 125.)*

According to Peale, a positive mind is empowered to think forward by creating *wonderful opportunities for winning*. This optimistic thinking engages and energizes. It instills confidence and confidence defeats self-doubt.

However, a BIG threat to thinking BIG is short-term thinking. This limiting thought process keeps the focus on today and confined to the present. It prevents seeing the BIG picture with tomorrow's possibilities.

Yet this doesn't mean *Forward Thinkers* neglect the small stuff. Taking care of details is critical when completing the puzzle of the BIG picture. As I said earlier, small consistent habits create extraordinary outcomes.

Thus, the key to successful bold and BIG thinking is balancing the small stuff with the BIG picture. Get the details done, but don't allow them to drain your energy or take your focus away from your future vision and path. Here are five tips for thinking BIG with positive results.[2]

Visualize the Impossible

What was impossible when I was a kid, is now possible and what is thought to be impossible today will be taken for granted tomorrow. In the decades since I was born, we went from princess phones to smartphones and now we have smartwatches.

Back in 1946, comic strip character Dick Tracy and his team wore two-way wrist radios. This inspired Martin Cooper to invent mobiles phone and later inspired smartwatches.[3]

This is an example of how yesterday's fantasy is now reality. What will be tomorrow's great invention? When you visualize the impossible, it may be one BIG thought away.

Don't Settle for the Obvious

The obvious is the easy way out of any dilemma. Yet the obvious traps you in today's thinking.

Escape from your mind's comfort zone. Free yourself from the bondage of the obvious and dare to think unconventional thoughts that go against the grain of today's thinking. You can't make a difference if you don't think differently.

History's greatest minds were ridiculed by small, minded people of their day. Don't care what they think; think BIG.

Be Open to Different Opinions

Expand your network of contacts with people in and outside your field of expertise. This empowers you to view the future from different perspectives.

Be open minded to different opinions, even when you don't agree. This stimulates civil and lively debate that sharpens the mind to defend or change your position. Stimulating thought from various angles keeps *Forward Thinkers* fresh. Differences of thought instill synergy. A well rounded paradigm looks at the future from all angles of the prism of reality.

Welcome Surprises

Even the best prepared *Forward Thinkers* will face unforeseen challenges and unexpected events on their journey. Yet these surprises can be a catalyst for new discoveries.

Insulin, penicillin, and warfarin were all discovered by accident. Instead of looking at a challenge as an obstacle, think of it as an opportunity to discover something new and incredible. A seemingly big roadblock can turn into a big discovery when you think BIG.

Keep it Real. Nothing But Net!

When you read my motivational book, *Go the Extra Yard: Empower the Champion Within You,* you learn that my passion for sports far exceeds my athletic ability. In fact, as I mentioned, I am spastic.

Basketball was one of my favorite sports to play as a youth. In a pickup game, when I got the ball in my hands, I envisioned me being the next NBA superstar.

In my mind's eye I dribbled to my left, then to my right. With a perfect behind the back dribble, I faked out my opponent. I was free to take an open jump shot from behind the three-point line.

In slow motion, I saw the ball leaving my hand and floating in a perfect arc toward the basket. Swish. It entered the center of the basket with NOTHING BUT NET.

However, let's get real. When I put my hands on the ball, I usually lost it out of bounds for a turnover.

To keep your BIG ideas from being lost out of bounds, make sure your BIG thinking is not outside of your talent level. Think BIG but KEEP IT REAL. Before you handle the ball of ideas, understand your strengths and weaknesses as well as the resources needed to achieve your BIG ideas. Then set realistic boundaries.

Otherwise, they will be thrown away with your daydreams. Stay in bounds with your outside the box thinking.

BIG Goals Get Bigger When Written

"Think little goals and expect little achievements. Think big goals and win big success," David Joseph Swartz said.

The Fifth Secret of the *12 Life-changing Secrets to Pop to the Top* is S.O.A.R. *High with Your Goals.* The acronym stands for Seek your Objective and Achieve your Reward. Achieving goals doesn't only get you to the top; it keeps you there.

Sadly, many people who haven't smelled the popcorn of success confuse goals with wishful thinking. Forward thinking is not daydreaming. It's a sound process of creating a vision of tomorrow that is attainable with realistic written goals.

As stated in *Smell the Popcorn*, a goal is a realistic and obtainable dream or objective of future prosperity, success, significance, or security. It must be attainable, measurable, accountable, and motivational. A goal should be written and have an action plan designed for obtaining the expected rewards within a specific success time (deadline).

> Goals shape and define the mission of our destiny.

Goals shape and define the mission of our destiny. In fact, without written goals that are focused and empowered by an achievement plan, our future is often determined by our past conditioning or luck.

Written goals make a big difference in achieving success as I mentioned in my book *Smell The Popcorn*.

In 1979, a study was conducted on Harvard MBA students to determine the impact of setting goals. This study showed only three percent of the students had written goals with action plans while 13 percent had unwritten goals and 84 percent had no defined goals.[4]

Ten years later, Mark McCormack, the author of *What They Don't Teach You in Harvard Business School*, conducted a follow-up study. According to McCormack, the three percent, who had written goals, earned an average of ten times more than the other 97 percent while the 13 percent, who had unwritten goals, earned an average of twice as much as the 84 percent without goals.[5]

You don't need a degree from Harvard to realize this study showed the importance of having written goals with action plans.

BIG Thinking + *WOW* Thinking = Results

New clothes for the twins, a new scanner for dad, and of course, a new dress for mom were at the top of the shopping list of the Marshall Family. Now that the wish list was complete, mom, dad, and the teenagers, Mark and Marsha, boarded the SUV for the short trip to the mall.

On the way, while the parents were discussing their shopping strategy, the twins were thinking about the fun arcade.

In no time at all, they arrived at their destination. Like always, it was hard to find a spot to park. Dad dropped off mom and the kids at the entrance while he searched for the ideal parking spot.

During the wait for dad, mom usually gave the twins $20.00 each to spend even though she knew these funds would be spent in less than an hour at the arcade.

This time, however, instead of $20.00, mom gave each twin $40.00. Both teenagers asked in unison, "Thanks, but why $40.00?" Mom explained since they are now thirteen-years old, they must learn how to prudently handle their own finances.

Both twins told their mom they would handle their finances well and would save most of their treasure for a later date. With a quick wave goodbye, both kids ran to the fun arcade. Mom yelled, "Meet us at the food court at noon. Love you! See you in two hours."

When the twins arrived at the mall's fun arcade, Mark immediately started playing his favorite games while Marsha looked around in deep thought. She was calculating her options.

How much should she spend here? Before she could even decide, Mark had spent a few dollars playing on one of the pinball machines.

Since Marsha didn't want to be tempted, she left the arcade and started walking to the shop that sold accessories for smartphones. On the way, she decided to save all her money to eventually buy the new smartphone case she wanted.

"If mom gives me money each time we go to the mall, I can save it and buy the case in a few weeks," she thought.

When Marsha walked into the shop, she discovered the case she wanted was marked 40% off. Instead of $60.00, it was on sale for $36.00 plus tax. This meant Marsha, who kept all her money, was able to purchase the smartphone case for less than $40.00.

At noon, the family met at the designated area. Mom and Dad wore looks of accomplishments while Marsha was smiling and Mark wore a frown since he spent all his money at the arcade.

"You look happy, what's up?" dad asked Marsha.

Marsha said, "I bought the phone case I wanted."

Mark interjected, "You couldn't. It costs $60.00."

Marsha explained her smartphone case was on sale. Since she didn't spend a penny at the arcade, unlike her brother, she was able to purchase the case she wanted.

This experience taught Marsha these important lessons regarding how BIG thinking plus WOW thinking equals results:

- Think BIG and don't settle for today's small stuff;
- Sacrifice today for a BIG reward tomorrow;
- Focus on BIG goals and not on meaningless desires;
- Managing resources is a BIG thing; and
- Sometimes success happens quicker than expected.

Don't Worry; Make It Happen

"Imagination creates reality," Richard Wagner said.

Stop worrying. Stop thinking, "I'm never going to get that job." Stop telling yourself, "I'm never going to get out of debt." Stop saying, "I'm never going to find someone to love me."

Don't worry about all that.

Replace worry with the WOW of thinking BIG.

When you think like that, you don't have to worry about when it's going to happen. It will happen!

Greatness happens when you think B.I.G. and think W.O.W.!

All limitations are self-imposed.

-Oliver Wendall Holmes

Take the Path Less Travelled

"Do not go where the path may lead, go instead
where there is no path and leave a trail."

- Ralph Waldo Emerson

3

Where Are You Going?

Several years ago, I was scheduled to give a training presentation to a small group of insurance agents. The meeting was held at a hotel near the New Orleans Airport.

On the day of the event, I went to the front desk of the hotel, introduced myself, and asked one of the associates for directions to the meeting room where I would be speaking.

The associate looked at me with a smile, pointed toward my left, and said, "Walk down this main hallway to the first corner. Here you take a right and walk down the corridor. When it ends, turn left and go to the last door on your left."

She paused, as if to admit the directions were confusing and cheerfully said, "Better yet, I'll take you there."

With her leading the way, I followed. During our walk, the associate asked, "What are you going to talk about?"

I said, "I'm talking on how to get to the top of your success."

"Interesting," she said without any further comment.

Finally, our journey ended with the associate saying, "Here you are. This is the room. Just go through this door."

"Thank you," I said. "By the way, would you like to attend my presentation? I'll teach you how to get to the top of your success."

The associate replied with a chuckle, "I'm not sure. How are you going to guide me to the top of my success when you can't even find your way to your meeting room?"

Her words were true. We are often so focused on getting to our destination that we forget to plan the course to get us there. When this happens, we lose track of our purpose and our vision becomes distorted.

After all, how can we plot a course for a significant future when we don't know where we are on our journey?

To find directions on an app, you need both a starting point and an end point. Otherwise, you can't create an accurate map.

Without a map, you are lost with no direction. When you're lost, you can't stay on course since you can't plot your course.

In other words, to discover your vision you must first know where you are before you can get to where you want to go. This fact isn't only important to reach the top. It's significant to stay there. The key to success is choosing the right path.

The Road Less Traveled

The phrase "the road less traveled" from M. Scott Peck's book of the same name refers to a traveler's decision to take or create an uncertain and unconventional path in lieu choosing the established and well-known ones. This critical selection symbolizes the pivotal life-changing choices that need to be made at various times during the journey of life.

When it comes to *Forward Thinkers*, this phrase applies since the fruition of their vision is seldom found on the popular route. As a result, these purpose driven pioneers trailblaze the path less taken to seek their vision (*Pop to the Top*™) and perpetuate their destiny (*Stay at the Top*™).

Yet to live a purpose driven life, you need to know where your purpose is driving you. Therefore, before starting your journey, you need to find your way with the equivalent of an inclusive travel brochure *(Vision Statement)* and an updated roadmap with flexible directions *(Fluid Mission Statement)*.

These documents prepare you for the road that leads to the top and the future route that empowers you to remain at the top.

Make Your Statements Count

Vision Statement[1] (Focused on the Future)

An inspirational and empowering *Vision Statement* (like a travel brochure) not only specifies where you are going, it defines who you are and your purpose for making the journey. The benefits and ultimate impact found at the destination are also stated along with the resources and contributors needed to make a successful trip.

A well-conceived *Vision Statement* gives life to the destination. It balances your goals, roles, and expectations with your personal and professional core values by aligning your vision with the mission.

Mission Statement[2] (Focused on the Present)

In comparison, a captivating, influential, and motivational *Mission Statement* (roadmap) gives clear, accessible, and precise directions on how to get to your destination. Like all good maps, it creates a sense of realism to the journey by identifying landmarks, assets, and possible obstacles.

In addition, a *Mission Statement* connects your goals, roles, and expectations with available resources and contributing partners in a set timeframe. As a fluid (flexible) statement, it provides alternate routes should an unpassable roadblock get in the way of your journey.

A personal statement is needed to guide a person through the various aspects of life while a corporation needs multiple statements for each department that is customized for their specific role (journey).

Three Statements to Stay on Course

The *Vision Statement* (purpose) and *Mission Statement* (path) serve as reference points for accountability that keep you on track.

In addition, I advise creating a *Value Statement*[3] (Principles). As the name suggests, it states the core values of your culture and your commitment to follow them.

According to John Maxwell, these values "authentically describe your soul." They keep you and your team grounded and serve as a reference point to bring you back to the right path if you go astray.

Every significant journey needs three galvanizing documents.

Define Your Path to Seek Your Vision

All great journeys start with a vision. Thus the first statement to create is your *Vision Statement*.

Writing an exceptional *Vision Statement* takes time, critical thinking, and lots of preparation. It's not something you throw together in a single meeting with nice sounding positive words.

Much of the wisdom and self-awareness needed to create a beneficial statement becomes clear by applying the *12 Life-changing Secrets* with the *Seven Significant Truths*. This insight empowers you to stay true to yourself while keeping true to the vision. Truth defines your path.

While in the developmental stage, make sure your statement clearly describes the key elements of your journey and connects to the overall mission while adhering to your core values.[4] As stated, your values keep the vision grounded with truth and not distorted with false expectations. If this isn't done, you and all who share your journey will become lost and disoriented even with a good *Mission Statement*.

As a guide to assist you in creating your document, the following who, what, where, when, and why questions[5] provide direction to get you started. The seventh question is optional since establishing timeframes can be set in either the *Vision Statement* or *Mission Statement*.

- Who are you? *(Self-awareness)*
- Why do you want to do this? *(Your purpose)*
- Where are you going? *(Destination)*
- What direction will you take?
  (Path to resources and contributors)
- Who do you serve? *(Benefit)*
- What is the impact? *(Result)*
- *OPTIONAL* – When will it happen?
  (Timeframe)

Aligning the Essential
Elements of the Vision Statement[6]

The graphic below illustrates how the six questions and optional seventh are aligned to create your empowering *Vision Statement* by keeping your core values at the center of the process.

"A statement of vision is the overarching purpose, the big dream, the visionary concept - something presently out of reach - so stated that it excites the imagination and challenges people to work for something they do not yet know how to do, " Robert K. Greenleaf said.

Aligning the Essential
Elements of the Mission Statement[7]

Seven essential elements for a captivating *Mission Statement* that aligns with your *Vision Statement* and *Value Statement*.

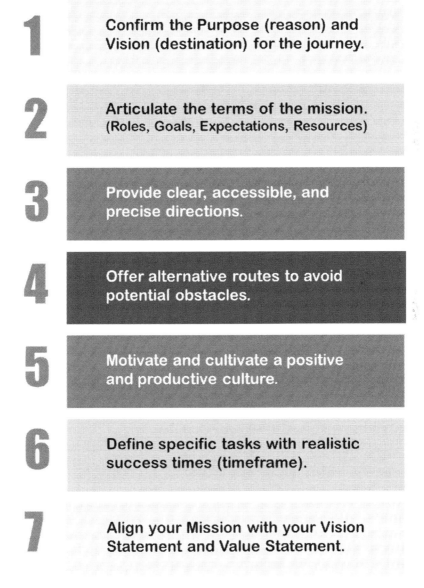

1 Confirm the Purpose (reason) and Vision (destination) for the journey.

2 Articulate the terms of the mission. (Roles, Goals, Expectations, Resources)

3 Provide clear, accessible, and precise directions.

4 Offer alternative routes to avoid potential obstacles.

5 Motivate and cultivate a positive and productive culture.

6 Define specific tasks with realistic success times (timeframe).

7 Align your Mission with your Vision Statement and Value Statement.

Steps to Follow the Path Less Taken

Forward Thinkers understand that despite the best preparation and planning, unexpected scenarios happen. Sometimes a minor detour is necessary but sometimes a major roadblock my result in a sizeable change in the path. Yet, no matter the circumstances, they know how to find joy in the adventure.

The following steps equip *Forward Thinkers* to joyfully stay on the best path possible without distractions, burden, and doubt.

- Seek the truth. *(Trust provides accurate direction.)*
- Get rid of emotional baggage. *(Lighten the load.)*
- Permanently delete your junk email. *(Don't litter.)* (Negative Thoughts, doubt, and negative messages.)
- Follow your guide. *(Stay on Path.)*
- Don't give up! *(Keep the faith and enjoy the ride.)*

Seek the truth. (Trust provides accurate direction.)

If you truly desire to *Stay at the Top*™, you must have a solid foundation anchored by the cornerstone of integrity. A cornerstone is a large immovable stone that sets the direction for the entire building.

Likewise, the cornerstone of integrity is the focal point of your inner character's foundation. It provides the depth and strength of character to follow your path without being tempted to stray on the road of self-destruction.

Integrity begins internally. You start by being true to yourself and genuine to others.

Therefore, integrity serves as your compass for right and wrong. It instils the trust that leads in the right direction.

Forward Thinkers build on the cornerstone of integrity, instead of trying to budge it by distorting the truth.

Get rid of emotional baggage. (Lighten the load.)

One of my friends had so much emotional baggage that when he flew on an airplane, the airlines charged him a baggage fee.

Seriously, our emotional baggage weighs us down. Our journey to success has enough challenges. We don't need to bring our own mental garbage to burden us.

The emotional baggage from the past, caused by guilt or pain, creates an unnecessary mental burden that drains our positive energy. This negative mindset prevents the development of new ideas, restricts imagination, and stops creativity since it forms a blockage caused by anger, frustration, and lack of forgiveness.

It's time to take that old baggage filled up with lots of junk and throw it into the dumpster of past failures. Put it out with the rest of the garbage that tries to you knock you off course. When you focus ahead on your vision, you can't see the trash you left behind.

Get rid of emotional baggage every day when you *Rise and Shine* (First Truth). It's time to forgive, forget, and forge ahead!

Permanently delete your junk email. (Don't litter.)

(Negative thoughts, doubt, and negative messages.)

Author and evangelist Joel Osteen teaches when a negative message comes your way, you need to delete it just like you delete junk email.

If someone unfairly criticizes you, hit delete. If someone fosters doubt, hit delete. If someone belittles you, hit delete. Press the delete button in your mind and say goodbye. Good riddance.

Don't waste another second of your precious journey with doubt. Delete the negative thought.

But I say do more. Make sure you delete negative thoughts for good. To get rid of them forever (permanently), take another step, like deleting emails. Once you deleted them the first time, you need to go the trash (junk) folder of your mind and hit delete all.

Now comes the final task. When your brain says do you want to permanently delete this junk, say, "Yes. I choose to permanently delete all negative thoughts, doubt, and negative messages that have clogged my mind far too long."

When anything negative appears, hit DELETE, DELETE, and YES DELETE.

Follow Your Guide (Stay on path.)

When going on an excursion to a new location, it's important to have an experienced guide to show you the way. Ideally, you should select a guide (mentor) who has successfully traveled the path less taken.

In addition to keeping you on the right path, your mentor keeps you focused on your vision (destination), holds you accountable, and makes the journey a joyful learning experience. A seasoned guide may also know shortcuts, rest stops, and how to avoid potential roadblocks.

However, make sure your guide is mentoring you on your path less taken and not trying to dictate you to take his (her or their) journey.

Don't Give Up. (Keep the faith and enjoy the ride.)

Forward Thinkers stay on path by keeping the faith with joy in their hearts. They know that anything of significance takes time. Even when results aren't happening right away, they don't get discouraged and lose their joy. They find joy in the moment.

Forward-thinking *Difference Makers*, people of significance, know greatness doesn't happen overnight. It takes work, determination, and patience. But most of all, it takes faith to start your seeds (kernels) of success popping. When you keep the faith, they will POP.

After all, most of the kernels in a microwave bag of popcorn don't POP until the last minute.

Don't give up. Keep POPPING and savour your popcorn while you enjoy the ride.

"Two roads diverged in a wood and
I took the one less traveled by,
and that has made all the difference."
-Robert Frost

What path will you to take?

Strike Up the Band

Leadership with an Organic Approach to DEI
Make What Makes You Different,
Make a Difference

"It is not a band. It is an idea."

- Gerard Way

4

Maestro Leadership:
Coming Together in Perfect Harmony

An orchestra consists of many different types of musical instruments with a wide range of distinct sounds. The conductor understands that without including one of the instruments, the song would not sound right.

Additionally, the conductor must often deal with musicians who come from diversified backgrounds and cultures. Some don't speak the same language. Yet all speak the same language when it comes to reading music.

Just like forming a symphony orchestra, when people gather either professionally or socially, the group usually consists of a diversified group with each member's contribution important to the success of the outcome/relationship.

Like a maestro, *Forward Thinkers* strike up their band of people with four distinct movements. With the skill of a virtuoso, they orchestrate a culture that harmonizes diversity, equity, and inclusion into a unified vision of a masterpiece.

Although, the qualities, functions, and techniques that make a conductor a maestro are successful in music, all are applicable to enhancing the performance of leadership at any level.

Your team is waiting for you to STRIKE UP THE BAND!

Four Movements of Classical Music

In music composition, a movement is a musical piece with its own form, key, tone, and mood usually performed as part of a much larger composition. Since a movement often contains a complete resolution or ending, a movement can be played as a standalone piece.[1]

However, to experience the full intended impact of the composition, as written, all movements must be performed in order.

Classical music is mostly performed in four distinct movements.[2] Each has its own purpose. Yet those purposes don't only apply to musicians. They apply to any form of effective leadership.

Opening Movement

The first movement is usually bright and upbeat. The conductor sets the tone with excitement for the entire composition.[3]

In business, this is when effective leadership establishes the groundwork for a positive, inclusive, and transparent culture. Excitement for the vision is generated. The importance of unity is stressed.

Second Movement

Usually slow and sedate are the characteristics of the second movement.[4]

This is the time for business leaders to slow down for monitoring progress without stopping momentum. It's a period of adjustments.

Third movement

A time to get up and move is part of the third movement. This can take the form of a dance.[5]

Everyone needs a break to recharge their excitement and rekindle passion. This is the time to celebrate the victories obtained up to this point. This joyful celebration reinforces the commitment for the final push.

Final Movement

Strong, triumphant, and assertive, often with repeating sections is the highlight of the fourth movement.[6]

This is the time to experience the joy and significance of success. It's also time to instill the desire to repeat the victory.

The Sounds of Diversity (Harmony)

In the 1920s the big band sound started to evolve by adopting the rhythms and combining the musical elements of ragtime, black spiritual, blues, and Latin music. Duke Ellington, Ben Pollack, Don Redman, and Fletcher Henderson were some of the more nationally popular big bands of the time.[7]

> The musical infusion… was an example of the amazing results shaped by diversity, equity, and inclusion.

The musical infusion of this progressive period was an example of the amazing results shaped by diversity, equity, and inclusion. It created many opportunities for talent from around the world to come to the United States.

'Prof,' as he was latter called by his students, left his home in Spain to find his *Popcorn Destiny* in America. The gifted Hispanic pianist with a Latin flair quickly became a band leader. Known for his syncopated Latin rhythms and unique sound, Prof's band was extremely popular during this big band era.

Yet things were suddenly about to change for the popular and forward thinking maestro. A hand injury he sustained in an auto accident ended his days as a band leader.

As a result, he moved from the East Coast to New Orleans where he dedicated his life to teaching music with the same passion and gusto he displayed as a performer.

For more than 10 years, I studied guitar with Prof, who was at times more of a surrogate grandfather than a music teacher.

It was during my lessons that he often shared his memories about being a band leader in the *Roaring Twenties*, which he described as a renaissance period for music.

"Back then, when it came to music, it was anything goes," Prof said with his Spanish accent.

Sparked by a surging economy, the prudish ways from the past were replaced with a loosening of social morality. Flappers redefined the modern look for American women while Jazz bloomed at this time.[8]

Getting the Band Together

It's important to note that before diversity, equity, and inclusion (DEI) were mainstream, Prof's leadership approach implemented all three. As a band leader, it didn't matter what a person looked like, how they spoke, or what they believed, if they were a great musician, he wanted them in his band.

He judged them on the level of talent and character. According to Prof, his band members not only included people from all over America, but also from around the world. His musicians came from Mexico, Africa, Ireland, Italy, and his home country of Spain.

They spoke in many tongues with many dialects, but all

spoke the language of music. Prof's unbiased and inclusive hiring (gathering) method formed a diversified and an amazingly popular band. All members, no matter black or white, young or old, had the same opportunity to excel. What made them different, made the difference.

Prof created an organic[9] approach to DEI that he used a century ago. It resulted in a melting pot of innovative sound that made his band one of the top groups on the East Coast.

In *Smell The Popcorn*, I compared his approach to making a pot of filé gumbo. The recipe for gumbo includes adding many different types of ingredients that are stirred together by the chef to create its unique delicious flavor.

Usually, the more you put into the pot, the tastier it gets. To add flavor to the band (team), start stirring the pot with diversity. Although commonalties are the catalyst to start the bonding, it's the differences that add zest to the journey.

When it comes to putting together your band, be blind to any differences. Like Prof, use his equitable approach to gathering talent. His performance-based method resulted in forming a diversified and inclusive band with everyone earning the opportunity to grow and excel. It was solely based on each member's unique gift of talent.

Make what makes you different, make a difference.

NOTE: Organic DEI starts by identifying DIVESITY as a FACT. People are different with unique talents, skills, gifts, and challenges. The PROCESS FOR DIVESITY is the task (ACT) of bringing an assorted group of people together to provide equal opportunities through the PRACTICE OF INCLUSION. The PROCESS FOR DIVERSITY and the PRACTICE OF INCLUSION are rooted in an unbiased state of mind that is the conviction of EQUITY. However, INCLUSION is ultimately an individual's CHOICE to participate.

Prof's Organic Triangle Approach to DEI

Emphasize Equity

When Prof formed his band, he selected people based on their musical talent and character.

Encourage Inclusion

To showcase the melting pot of sound, Prof chose arrangements that gave all members the opportunity to be featured performers.

Embraced Diversity

Prof knew to create a unique sound needs uniquely exceptional musicians who are given the freedom to be themselves.

DIVERSITY PROCESS

The process for diversity is defined as bringing together a group of people from various backgrounds. Usually it refers to age, race, gender, sexual preference, nationalities, and religious beliefs.[10]

EQUITY

Equity is the quality of being impartial, reasonable, and fair. It means not being judgmental.[11]

VISION
Leadership
SYNEGY

INCLUSION

Inclusion is the practice or policy of providing equal access to opportunities and resources for people who might otherwise be excluded.[12]

Vibrant Vision

DEI enables the art of leadership to paint a more vibrant picture of the vision, since there are more colors and brushes to work with.

Crescendo, Diminuendo, and Pause

Prof wasn't only a popular band leader, gifted musician, and an award-winning music teacher, his varied experiences made him a wise philosopher. I learned much about music and life from Prof, which I shared in many of my other books.

Prof was the first person to introduce me to the similarities between a maestro and a successful forward thinking leader in any field.

Examples of this comparison include a maestro's use of Crescendos *(gradual increase in loudness)*, Diminuendos *(decrease in loudness)*, and the Pause *(sudden moment of silence)* in a musical composition.

The Crescendos and The Diminuendos

MAESTRO: A maestro knows how to effectively utilize crescendos and diminuendos to enhance the experience of a musical performance. When used properly, both add to the intensity of the composition.

LEADER: In the same way, a successful leader recognizes when it's time to bring out the best in someone and when to hold them back. When used correctly, this maximizes a person's performance.

The Powerful Pause

MAESTRO: For a maestro, the most powerful act that makes the most impact is the pause. This sudden and abrupt moment of silence serves as a musical punctuation mark. It creates the feeling that something is going to happen. It creates suspense and expectations.

LEADER: A great leader also appreciates the power of the pause. There are times during the mission that leaders must stop and pause the momentum to ensure everyone is on the right path. This is a timeout to refocus, refresh, recommit, and make adjustments as needed for the rest of the journey. However, unlike the maestro, the leader uses the pause to eliminate suspense and clarify expectations.

It doesn't matter if you are the leader of the band of musicians or the leader of the team of achievers or misfits, these tools are highly effective in enriching the performance of the band or team.

A Band with Character

Prof knew it took an unbiased and forward thinking leader with unique characteristics to bring a talented and diverse group of people together and to keep them together. Although there are many skills and characteristics needed for exceptional leadership at any level and in any industry, these are my seven core characteristics of a forward thinking (band) leader.

Communication - Unlike managers who inform their followers of only need-to-know-facts, effective leaders are powerful communicators who successfully use *communication* to unify their diversified team members.

Through expressing equity and inclusion, leaders engage members to firmly commit to the mission, vision, and shared values. Successful communication is key for bringing the diversified team (band) together in perfect harmony. *(More about communication on page 69.)*

Competence - People won't follow anyone who lacks *competence*. Leaders earn respect and credibility through accomplishments and a record of being fair, impartial, and nonjudgmental. Competent leaders have a thorough understanding of the process as a whole and are aware of specific individual assignments. *Competence* is seeing the BIG picture without forgetting the small.

Connection – Effective leaders use unbiased empathy to connect with their team. They harmonize the vision (purpose) and the mission (path) with values (principles). This *connection* unites the right people at the right time with the right resources for the right reasons.

Confidence - *Confidence* inspires *confidence*. People are drawn toward people who exhibit *confidence*. Great leaders initiate, nurture, and perpetuate a positive, energetic, and confident culture through inspiration, motivation, and engagement while avoiding conceit, arrogance, and inflated egos.

Consistency - Stability, dependability, and reliability are the result of consistent behavior. *Consistency*, when combined with honesty, transparency, and integrity, builds trust and instills a sense of security.

Creativity – The vision of effective leaders flows from their creative perspective. *Creativity* empowers innovation, change, and adaptability. A key to success in music is the conductors' creative ability to change musical keys to best highlight the talent of the performer.

Captivate – Effective leaders are magnetic. They attract diverse people to come together for a common vision. They understand how to use their magnetism to *captivate*, engage, and inspire followers without abusing authority.

12 Notes of Wisdom to Strike Up the Band

As mentioned earlier, there are similarities between the functions of a maestro and the actions of a successful leader in any field. Here are twelve of the most common that can be applied to music and any professional organization. *Business equivalent in parenthesis.*

- Set the tempo, tone, and the dynamics of the song (*workplace*).
- Recruit new members to fill a specific instrument (*job*).
- Allow soloists (*each team member*) the freedom to improvise.
- Teach new songs (*assignments*) by guiding each section (*group or department*) through their parts (*roles*).
- Instruct band (*team*) members when to play (*take charge*) during a song (*project*).
- Monitor rehearsals (*activity*) to identify areas to improve.
- Organize and schedule rehearsals (*assignments*) as needed.
- Select the music (*projects*) that best fits the band's (*team's*) talent.
- Arrange the score (*role*) to match the band's (*team's*) skill level.
- Ensure that all musicians (*team members*) feel included.
- Get feedback from the band (*team*) for ways to improve.
- Do the ordinary extraordinarily well.

Communication is Vital to Diversity

The journey to success is seldom walked alone. That's why we all need a band of people to contribute to the success of our journey.

For Prof and other past and current band leaders, musical notes provide the common denominator for communication. After all, music is the universal language. Yet with verbal communication, people who speak the same language often miscommunicate.

Everyone is different in the way they perceive the world. To establish a culture that bands together a diversified group, the leader recognizes through empathy the various individual perspectives. Empathy unites and harmonizes the multiple monologues into dialogues of synergy. This is communication at its finest.

Effective verbal communication isn't an easy task. Anyone can speak but few people have developed the skill to become a great communicator. It takes work to converse. As a result, managers *(they manage things; not people)*, who are not leaders, often take it easy by conducting so-called dialogues that are simultaneous monologues.

A monologue results when one or more parties of a potential conversation aren't serious about speaking or listening. In contrast, a successful dialogue makes a great conversation.

Successful dialogues occur when the speaker speaks with what I refer to in *Smell the Popcorn* as adding S.P.I.C.E. to the conversation. In this communication style, all parties listen with empathy. Empathy enables a listener to understand the speaker's unique perspective.

The acronym S.P.I.C.E. stands for Simplicity, Personality, Imagination, Connection, and Entertainment to our messages. *(Secret 8 in Smell the Popcorn)*

When both speakers/listeners converse in this productive fashion, a conversation develops as soon as both listeners understand the message by listening with empathy and responding accordingly. This is the ideal path to orchestrate a harmonious conversation. *(See Appendix E on page 129.)*

Once effective communication is established, relationships can start to develop. This empowers the connection to perfection. *(Secret 9 in Smell the Popcorn.) (See Appendix F on page 131.)*

Things aren't Always the Way They Appear

Sally, a junior partner of a large law firm, often worked late to complete her legal research. However, tonight she needed to take the bus home since her car was in the repair shop.

As she leaves the downtown office building, the deserted street frightens Sally. She didn't realize how dark and lonely this part of town was at this time of night. Instead of returning to the office to call a cab, Sally becomes adventurous and proceeds onward.

As she continues her journey, she notices a tall thin man with an unkempt beard and long stringy hair. This shabbily dressed stranger appears to be following her. Since she is frightened by his appearance, she starts to walk faster. But as she quickens her pace, so does the suspicious stranger. Sally is now convinced that he is following her. The pace continues for several blocks.

Finally, to her relief, Sally arrives at the bus stop. The group of people already waiting includes a teenager, an elderly woman, and a well-dressed businessman.

She decides to stand next to the businessman for protection and starts a conversation. The suspicious stranger begins to pace the ramp and, on several occasions, comes extremely close to Sally.

After several minutes, the bus arrives. Sally sits in the rear of the bus so she can observe the other riders. The teenager, stranger, and businessman sit in the middle, while the elderly woman sat in front.

After a few minutes into the ride, Sally wonders if that stranger stole her wallet when he walked by her. She quickly swung her purse on her lap and noticed that it was open, and her wallet was gone. Anger overcomes her fear as she stands to yell, "He stole my wallet."

Upon hearing her screams, the shabby stranger jumps out of his seat and runs into the aisle. About the same, the businessman also jumps up and runs into the aisle. Suddenly, the shabby stranger tackles the businessman and throws him on the floor of the bus. He immediately puts handcuffs on the well-dressed man. A search of his coat pockets produces a lady's black leather wallet.

"Lady, is this your wallet?" asked the longhaired man.

Sally hesitantly shook her head in confirmation.

"I'm sorry that I frightened you before, but I'm an undercover cop. Since a lot of crime is going on in this area, I decided to follow you," proclaimed her protector.

"I had a tip this guy was stealing wallets," he said.

Sally's perception of reality was totally wrong. She allowed her predetermined biased mindset, by which she judges people, to be based on appearance only. Thus, the person who she thought meant harm was her protector.

On the other hand, the well-dressed man that she assumed to be a businessman was a thief.

In an instant, she took a paradigm leap. Instead of an evil grungy crook, the shabbily dressed man is now seen as her hero. In a second, he went from being an ugly frog to becoming the knight in shining armor.

Organic DEI Lessons regarding choosing the right band (team) members.
- Keep OBJECTIVE! Predetermined paradigms distort the view.
- Don't let DIFFERENCES make you indifferent.
- Stop DEEP-ROOTED BIAS from affecting your decision making.
- Look beyond the external façade to discover the CORE CHARACTER.
- TRUST is not based on appearance.
- SUCCESS can be found with unexpected people.

"Without music, life would be a mistake."
-Friedrich Nietzsche

Truth #5

Make a Difference;
Not Excuses

Accountable Leadership in Action

"If your presence doesn't make an impact,
your absence won't make a difference."

- Trey Smith

5

A Tribute to an American Hero
Who Made a Difference; Not Excuses

In 1972, as a captain in the United States Marine Corps, Richard I. "Butch" Neal served as the *Senior Military Instructor* of my high school's JROTC program. Prior to this assignment, the future general served in the Vietnam War where he earned the Purple Heart, Silver Star, and Bronze Star for Valor.

Even as a young captain, he was a great leader and visionary. His vision was to make the Jesuit High School JROTC the best JROTC.

One of his many enhancements included creating a military band. However, he needed one more experienced drummer, like me, to make his band complete.

I was shocked when I was told to report to the JROTC office to talk with Capt. Neal since I elected physical education instead of military science. When I entered the room, he was sitting at his desk with a chest full of ribbons while retired sergeants stood on each side behind him. I knew something was up since the sergeants were smiling.

Capt. Neal, as an effective leader, passionately shared his vision and communicated his plan. He asked me to volunteer to join the band. This meant giving up my free period to attend JROTC classes, staying late after school to practice, and some weekend work since I was still part of the PE program. All for no grade.

You can't say no to great men who are great leaders. Capt. Neal was both. I promptly said YES! It was the best thing to happen to me.

During my senior year, which saw the Jesuit Marine Corps JROTC program become the best in the nation, Capt. Neal taught me how to compassionately serve with honor, to strategically plan to overcome setbacks, and to bravely lead with mental toughness and empathy. He taught his cadets how to live the Marine Corps' motto *Semper Fidelis*, which is Latin for "always faithful."

When it was time to turn in my Dress Blues at the end of my school year, I was told to report to the captain's office. He greeted me with a big smile. He said he wanted to personally say thank you for volunteering to make his vision become reality. He then proceeded to take the emblems off my uniform's hat and jacket. He placed them in a small box and said these unforgettable words:

"In life you will face many trials that seem hopeless. But when you do, look inside this box and remember the things you learned this past year. I know you will get through them and know that I will always consider you a Marine," the then Captain said.

I cannot tell you how many times I have looked inside that small box (always kept in the top drawer of my desk) and every time I gained strength from his words. I was honored to speak with him several months before he died. I told him about the story that features him in one of my books. I sent him a signed copy of my book and he sent me a signed copy of his book *What Now, Lieutenant*. I treasure it and the personal message he wrote to me inside the cover.

In 1998, Richard I. Neal retired as a four-star General and Assistant Commandant of the Marine Corps (ACMC).

Gen. Neal was a great man, leader, and mentor who achieved his *Popcorn Destiny*. He will be remembered for his bravery, leadership, and his high standard of excellence. The General made a difference but never made excuses.

Accountability began with him. His legacy won't be forgotten.

Thank you for turning this drummer boy into a man. His wisdom continues to inspire me today. I salute you. Rest in peace.

"When good men die, their goodness does not perish."
Euripides

Make a Difference
Eyeball Level Leadership

"A leader is one who knows the way, goes the way, and shows the way," John C. Maxwell said. General "Butch" Neal was all three.

When the then Capt. Neal took over the JROTC program at my high school, the decades old program was suffering from poor enrolment and low prestige. In fact, despite being the first established Marine Corps JROTC in the country, it was in trouble and was close to being thrown out by the school or pulled by the Marine Corps.[1]

The program needed a fixer. It needed "Butch" to fix things.

Due to his difference making leadership, the faltering program was named the number one Marine Corps JROTC in the country in his first year in command. He did with what he called *eyeball level leadership.*

"When the inspector general paid a visit to inspect the unit, he and his team were impressed with the turnaround of the unit and the excitement and *esprit de corps** of the young men," Gen. Neal recalled.[2]

"Our cadet corps was once again proud to wear the uniform, and the school loved our terrific drill team and our first-class band," he said.

This *Difference Maker* (fixer) used influential communication to connect with the cadets and clearly defined his vision along with clarifying the cadets' roles. His no non-sense and common-sense style of leadership made an immediate impact. He made a difference.

Capt. Neal was accountable to his cadets, and they were accountable to him and his staff. Earning respect was a two-way street.

When asked what made the difference to take the program from worst to first, he said, "It was just common-sense approach to leadership. We showed respect to the student while at the same time making sure that they understood our expectations of them and letting them know what they should expect from us. And that is *eyeball level leadership* at its finest."[3]

NOTE: Esprit de corps is a feeling of pride, fellowship, and common loyalty shared by the members of a particular group.

Gen. Neal's Keys to Make a Difference

The trials and dangers of fighting in a war cannot be compared to anything that I can imagine. I was fortunate not to experience the horrors of combat, but I respect those who serve, served, suffered, and in too many cases died for our freedom.

In his book *What Now, Lieutenant,* Gen. Neal gives a vivid account of his life both on and off the battlefield. However, it was during his tour of duty in Vietnam, the then lieutenant learned to be an effective hands-on leader with the following attributes:[4]

* **Common Sense** - The ability to perceive, understand, and communicate complicated issues from a perspective shared by nearly everyone while making sound practical decisions that are understood by all defines the term *common sense*. This was important to Gen. Neal.

* **Courageous -** The strength of a leader is defined by how he (she or they) responds with courage during times of challenges, adversities, setbacks, and controversies. *Courageous* leaders grow despite obstacles. They bravely accept the consequences for their actions and decisions. They aren't afraid to make the right decision even if it isn't popular.

* **Character –** The *character* of a respected leader is grounded by integrity. Good *character* is of utmost importance for a *Forward Thinker* when it comes to developing trust with those influenced. As I said, integrity is the cornerstone of success. Upon this solid rock, great leaders build the foundation of influential leadership.

- **Compassion** - Empathy in motion describes *compassion*. A compassionate leader shares the emotions of followers and desires to support them in overcoming any trials and celebrating the victories.

- **Conviction / Commitment** – "People don't follow words, they follow *conviction* and without *conviction* the words are meaningless," Jennifer Ott said. Gen. Neal's *conviction* (fervor) as a leader was totally committed to making a difference. In return, he expected from his team no less than the same level of *commitment* to the mission and its vision.

No Excuses (Accountability)
Responsibility and Accountability are Not the Same

Before implementing the techniques to create and cultivate a culture of accountability, *Forward Thinkers* need a solid understanding of what makes the words *accountability* and *responsibility* different. Although, these terms are often used interchangeably, they have a different emphasis.

Responsibility is focused on the task.[5]
Accountability is focused on the result.[6]

According to *the Center for Leadership Studies*, "accountability relates more to the results of a given task and carries with it a sense of ownership over those results."

Cultivate a Culture of Accountability

No one is perfect. Mistakes will happen. It's inevitable. Thus, the purpose of a *Culture of Accountability* is to remove the fear of making mistakes. This enables prompt responses to errors with corrective action before they manifest into something bigger.

Instead of sifting through the blame game and lame excuses, productive leadership spends its valuable time being proactive with solutions and not wasting energy conducting enquiries.

The emphasis is providing resolutions and not criticism. Initial mistakes are used as learning experiences and not yelling sessions.

These nine tips plant and cultivate a *Culture of Accountability*.[7]

1. Leadership Plants the Seeds by Setting Example[8]

The key to planting a successful *Culture of Accountability* lies solely with *influential leadership*.[9] Before anything else, influential leaders set the example by being accountable to themselves as well as the members of their teams.

By setting the stage, team members gain respect for and trust in leadership thereby becoming more eager to be accountable for their individual roles. Likewise, a manager who never admits to failing or making a mistake is setting a pattern for team members to do the same.

The next action taken by *influential leadership* for planting a *Culture of Accountability* are:

- Assign the right people for the right tasks.
- Provide training with appropriate resources.
- Clearly communicate the vision, tasks, roles, and goals.
- Define realistic expectations and set attainable success times (deadlines).
- Monitor progress for feedback.

When planting the seeds of accountability, it is imperative the team is well prepared. This means assigning the right people for tasks and responsibilities that correspond to their level of talent, expertise, and experience. Without a perfect match, failure is unavoidable.

Once the members are in the right fit, proper training along with appropriate resources are provided as needed based on an assessment of talent. If not trained and equipped with the tools for success, the mission fails. There is no need for accountability. Lack of leadership is to blame.

Communicating a clear vision with defined tasks, roles, and goals are imperative in creating a culture that is accountable to its mission. At this point, realistic expectations and clear success times (deadlines) are set and documented.

Progress is monitored with scheduled and impromptu discussions to get feedback from the frontline. Periodic dialogues identify what is working and what needs to change. These regular discussions ensure accountability on an ongoing basis.

2. Take Ownership and Accept Consequences[10]

In a *Culture of Accountability*, leaders and team members take ownership of their actions (or lack thereof) and accept the consequences. Both are assessed on the results of their decisions not their actions. Most unrepeated and unintentional errors are considered learning experiences with the focus on corrective action instead of extreme disciplinary recourse or verbal abuse.

3. Rooted on Truth, Honesty, and Transparency

Lies and coverups are still considered serious violations and the perpetrators will face serious consequences since the core of this culture is rooted on truth, honesty, and transparency.

Without integrity from leadership and its members, a *Culture of Accountability* will exist in name only.

4. Dealing with Real People not Business Theory

Keep in mind we are dealing with real people and real-life issues when implementing this culture. It's not a theoretical concept learned in business school nor is it a corporate feel-good experiment.

Cultivating a *Culture of Accountability* takes a lot of work to understand the people and how they individually relate to the process. A person's feelings and personality must be considered.

Yet establishing accountability is a wise investment of energy for *Forward Thinkers* who can't waste time with personality issues and "he said she said (they said)" scenarios of blame shifters.

5. Transformation Takes Time, Patience, Consistency

A *Culture of Accountability* takes time, patience, and consistency to develop. It's not an overnight transformation since it goes against basic human behavior to shift blame when accused of wrongdoing. Although, not instant, this culture is worth the investment of time.

6. The Devil Made Me Do It

Flip Wilson, a popular comic from the 70s, had this famous line in his comedy routines when accused of wrongdoing: "The devil made me do it."

After all, isn't it only natural for the big brother to blame his younger sibling for breaking mom's favorite vase?

Does this sound like you when you were a child? Were you the one being blamed or were you the blamer?

When the blame game starts, nip it in the bud before it grows into something ugly. Weed out the blame shifter. Go right to the source. Identify the reason and the truthfulness for the blamer's accusation and implement corrective action as needed. If this is a character flaw in the member, leadership must determine the next step.

7. Permission Granted[11]

Although members of this culture may interpret it as getting *Permission to Fail*, it is not giving permission to work less, not to work, or be careless. At this point members who are slacking aren't fully taking ownership of the results of their actions. They are failing.

In a *Culture of Accountability*, after an honest mistake is made, the only time you fail is when you fail to learn its lesson.

It is understandable that some things are out of the control of the member, but this is not an excuse for laziness or apathy. Abusers must be dealt with immediately in a compassionate and fair way.

Instead of *Permission to Fail*, *influential leadership* in a healthy *Culture of Accountability* gives permission (freedom) to be innovative self-starters. When all team members buy into the *Permission to Succeed* paradigm, positive change occurs that results in personal and corporate growth.

However, there is no room in this culture for deadweight slackers.

"The only real mistake is the one from which we learn nothing," Henry Ford said.

8. "I Got Your Back" Support[12]

In most reasonable cases, when a member makes an unintentional mistake, leadership needs to provide full support. To make a *Culture of Accountability* work, leadership must have an "I Got Your Back" mentality.

Giving people the opportunity to correct their mistakes and move forward allows them to learn and grow. It makes a big difference in the big picture when leadership provides support with correction not rejection.

In contrast, if the member feels unsupported by management, he (she or they) will make excuses, shift the blame, or start a coverup when a mistake is made.

In this scenario, the member did not fail; the leadership did.

9. Compassionate and Fair[13]

A primary reason that employees are reluctant to be accountable is fear. Some fear if they make a mistake, management will treat them unfairly and without compassion while others fear it would disappoint their manager and team or may result in them losing their job. In a well-established *Culture of Accountability* with strong leadership, this doesn't happen.

While leaders in this culture are compassionate and fair, they are not blind to abusers who take advantage of their sympathetic tone of leadership. Those who violate the culture are dealt with accordingly. When responding, avoid making rash decisions but be prudent in your judgment.

In addition, habitual careless mistakes and errors that cannot be addressed through training must be addressed by identifying the root cause. If unacceptable behavior continues and cannot change, the member, when possible, will be reassigned to other responsibilities.

The time is always right to do what is right.
-Martin Luther King

Avoid the *Ain't Dere No More* Syndrome

"The things you do for yourself are gone when you are gone, but the things you do for others remains your legacy."

- Kalu Ndukwe Kalu

6

Slide Rulers and Purple Signs

As I approach a significant high school reunion, I find myself reflecting on my teenage years when slide rulers were required in class and hand-held calculators were only available to the rich kids.

Decades ago, the big problems with students were chewing gum and smoking in the bathrooms. Now, instead of gum and cigarettes, teachers search kids for guns and knives.

In the early 70s, you could take a date to watch a movie at the outdoor drive-in. Then, after the flick, both of you could enjoy a couple of burgers, fries, and shakes at the Shoney's Big Boy for less than five bucks.

It was a time before cable TV and satellite dishes, when fuzzy screened televisions with antennas wrapped in tin foil could receive only four channels if you count PBS. But despite the limited networks, I found it harder to choose between the few shows of the 70s than the 100 plus programs of today. Looking back, I wished I had a VCR, but I had to wait several years before I could buy one.

Back then there were no iPhones, iPods, iPads, or iTunes. We didn't even have an IHOP in New Orleans. When you talked about "I," you were talking about yourself in the first-person singular nominative case.

The 70s were the zenith for Crescent City landmarks and icons such as K&B Drugstores, McKenzie's Bakery, Schwegmann Brothers Giant Supermarkets, and Rosenberg's Furniture Store at "1825 Tulane."

Speaking of Zenith, my family's TV was that brand. I remember watching WWL's Hap Glaudi with the sports and Nash Roberts with his grease pen giving the latest weather forecast. And who can forget Terry Flettrich, aka *Mrs. Muffin*, on the Midday Show with Wayne Mack, aka *The Great McNut*.

When I was in high school, you could "look on any corner and what do you see, a big purple sign that says friendly K&B." Like most New Orleans natives who were teenagers in the 70s, I recall the tune so well.

I still remember K&B's soda fountain area that served the best plain nectar sodas in the world. Pity, before it closed, these fountains of treats were turned into rows of magazine racks.

And speaking of dessert, I still crave a McKenzie's king cake, glazed donuts, and Dick Bruce's favorite custard pie.

Despite these fond memories, the 70s were a time of loss. Young men were dying in the jungles and swamps of Vietnam while Americans were trying to reason with a presidential scandal.

It was a time of uncertainty, much like it is today. It was a time for change. But to all my fellow graduating seniors, no matter if they lived in small towns or big cities, it was a time to dream. To dream about changing the world and making a difference. And for many, such as *Forward Thinker* Bill Gates, who graduated the same year as me, they did.

Reflection can be great. To recall the faces, names, and places of yesterday always brings me more smiles than tears.

It's good to think about the past. But life is about change. It's about growth and it's about learning.

This doesn't mean we should forget the past, but we cannot be trapped in it. Yesterday is gone. Many of the people and the places that made us who and what we are today exist only in some faded photographs and in our priceless memories.

To *Stay at the Top*™, *Forward Thinkers* learn from yesterday, live for today, and plan for tomorrow with outside the box thinking. Thus, to *Stay at the Top*™ it is time to move out of the old box filled with slide rulers and purple signs.

Think Forward! Don't Stink!

Forward thinking does not have an expiration date. It's a lifetime mindset that is part of a consistent routine. Forward thinking is a dynamic thought process that is perpetual. Once forward thinking is abandoned, the once fresh and progressive outlook will stagnate. As a result, even longtime successful *Forward Thinkers* will fail.

In prior truths, key roles and traits to *Pop to the Top*™ and *Stay at the Top*™ were offered. Now we look at what not to do.

There are several factors that corrupt, distort, and/or distract the vision of *Forward Thinkers*. Ego, greed, overconfidence, arrogance, and stubbornness are usually the root causes that blur the once fresh vision. This leads to bad decision making which leads to bad outcomes.

For others, time will take its toll. Some of these once *Forward Thinkers* will experience burnout or retire while others will face uncontrollable external events or lack resources, both financial and talent.

In many situations, stagnation occurs when future generations of leadership don't have the entrepreneur mindset, skills, and spirit to take the vision to the next level.

When any one of the above scenarios happens, even the most seasoned trendsetters are forced to make tough decisions to ensure perpetuation of the vision. If change is not made, the once prosperous vision will stagnate and fail.

Lessons from Case Studies

The easiest and best way to learn is from the mistakes of others. The hardest and most painful way is to learn from our own mistakes. The following case studies provide painless lessons gained from other people's mistakes.

Examples of three once highly successful organizations founded by *Forward Thinkers* that *Ain't Dere No More*[1] (as they say in New Orleans) are examined in this chapter.

The common denominator for failure for the first two case studies was the desire to grow outside their successful business model (vision). Unwise mergers and leveraged acquisitions financially doomed these once prosperous organizations.

The third's demise resulted from not adapting to the times.

In hindsight, when seeking guidance on expansion, these fallen risk taking *Forward Thinkers* should have listened to the words from the Kenny Rogers song the Gambler.

You got to know when to hold 'em, know when to fold 'em.
Know when to walk away and know when to run.

In contrast, the fourth positive case study presents a timeline of growth from one store to an international craze and the tough decision to take the next step at the right time.

Makin' Groceries

Schwegmann Brothers Giant Supermarkets[1] was a highly successful supermarket chain in the Greater New Orleans area for decades. It was started by a family lead by a *Forward Thinker*. Through innovation and planned growth, he developed a business model with a paradigm shift that the national chains could not compete with locally.

Instead of emphasizing financial return on sales (national chain concept), he and his partners emphasized financial return on investments. By using this paradigm, this out-of-the-box thinking resulted in average sales that were approximately double the national chains. This was unheard of when their first supermarket opened in 1946.

After decades of record growth, the *Forward Thinker* stepped down from his leadership role after suffering a stroke. His son purchased the grocery stores and became the chief executive officer.

A few years later, the current generation of leadership abandoned the company's historically successful blueprint for expansion. The new CEO leveraged the company to expand by acquiring another regional chain. This leadership decision was tainted by bad advice and miscalculations.

As a result, the once successful regional chain, started by a forward-thinking entrepreneur, closed in liquidation.

Who knows, if an updated version of the traditional route for expansion had been taken, families in the GNO may still be *makin' groceries*[2] at a Schwegmann Brothers Giant Supermarket.

I Love the Chicken[3]

"Love that chicken from Popeyes®," is a phrase to which I can relate. Ever since I ate my first piece of spicy chicken back in 1972, I was hooked.

Popeyes was founded by Al Copeland, who was a high school dropout. At 16, he went to work as a soda jerk at a supermarket but soon left to work at one of the *Tastee Donut* Shops owned by his older brother.

At 18, Copeland sold his car to buy one of his brother's donut shops. It was here that his forward thinking laid the seeds that would eventually grow into Popeyes.

More than 50 years ago, the young innovator realized that revelers at Mardi Gras were looking for fast carryout food to bring to the parade routes. He discovered there were very few options at the time. This inspired Copeland to fry chicken in one of his donut shop's deep fryers to sell to the parade goers. He saw a need and responded with a solution. This is a classic case of forward thinking.

It was such a hit that in 1972 Copeland opened a fast food chicken restaurant next to his donut shop. He called it *Chicken on the Run*. After a several months, the upstart restaurant unexpectedly closed.

But this *Forward Thinker* was resilient. His first attempt at being a restaurateur failed, but he wasn't a failure. He did not give up. Four days later, he reopened the place as *Popeyes Mighty Good Chicken* which evolved to a name change to *Popeyes Famous Fried Chicken* in 1975.

A year later, Copeland began franchising. Over the next 10 years around 500 outlets joined the family of franchisees.

Even though Popeye's was a huge success, the local boy from New Orleans with the bigger than life personality wasn't satisfied. Like many *Forward Thinkers*, his vision became distorted by outside influences that preyed on his ego. They fueled his quest to be number one even though they knew the plan was risky.

In 1989, Popeyes, the third-largest chicken chain, purchased Church's Chicken, the second largest. It was a decision that received much criticism. The ill-fated merger of these chicken chain giants resulted in competing locations and many other serious operational and logistic problems.

Despite efforts to address the numerous challenges caused by the merger, Al Copeland Enterprises, which operated both chains, was facing severe financial problems. The merger was heavily financed with the assets of both chains held as security.

In 1991, with about $400 million of debt, Copeland filed for Chapter 11 bankruptcy protection for his company. His quest to be the number one chicken chain ended in failure.

Although the franchise continues to thrive under the name of *Popeyes Louisiana Kitchen*, the man with BIG ideas was no longer in charge.

Al Copeland died in 2008, but his bigger than life legacy lives on. Looking back, Copeland should have listened to the sound thinking minds that were against the merger.

But no matter what, he won't be forgotten anytime soon. His philanthropy efforts continue to make an impact today.

The Fall of an American Staple[4]

As a kid, I remember walking with my grandmother to the Woolworth store not far from my home. The store offered a wide range of items from toys to household necessities, but my favorite spot was the restaurant area. The cheeseburgers were the best. The milkshakes were great too.

For more than a century, Woolworth was an American staple located in large and small shopping areas with an emphasis in the main downtown districts.

It started in 1879 when Frank Winfield Woolworth opened his first successful store. In the next few decades, the F.W. Woolworth Co. operated over 1800 stores throughout the United States, Canada, Britain, and three other foreign countries.

Woolworth was one of the first American retailers to make merchandise accessible to the shopping public without the assistance of a salesclerk. This type of forward thinking was revolutionary in the retail market at the time. This along with undercutting the prices of local merchants proved an unstoppable combination.

Growth continued. At the time of its centennial celebration (1979), the number of stores operated by Woolworth grew to over 4000 stores in the United States and abroad. However, things were about to change.

As American shoppers abandoned the Woolworth retail model and shifted to shopping at malls and big-box stores, Woolworth didn't try to compete.

Instead of adapting to the rapidly evolving world of retail, the leadership of the F.W. Woolworth Co. refused to change. The once forward thinking mentality that proved successful became outdated and stale.

Eventually time caught up with this once American staple. In 1997, Woolworth's closed its final U.S. locations.

The unwillingness of management to adapt by responding to new retail trends and implementing technology are considered the main reasons for failure.

The Smoothie Path to Success[5]

Back in the early 70s, Steve Kuhnau, a *Forward Thinker*, was very passionate about discovering a tasty way to stay healthy. This led him to experiment with blending various combinations of fresh fruits, yogurt, vitamins, and proteins to create great tasting and healthy smoothies. After trying many combinations, Kuhnau created several flavors of smoothies with a purpose.

His home-based experiments for a delicious healthy alternative proved to be a success. Thus, Smoothie King® was born.

In 1973, Steve Kuhnau and his wife opened their first smoothie bar in a suburb of New Orleans. I remember getting an *Angel Food* smoothie at that location and loving every sip. I was hooked. It's still one of my favorites.

Sixteen years after the first smoothie bar was opened, Smoothie King® Franchises, Inc. was formed. What began as a passionate experiment in Kuhnau's home was now becoming an international phenomenon.

Over the next three decades, Smoothie King® rapidly expanded across America. The term *smoothie* had become a household word synonymous with good health, quality, and wellness.

In 2012, Wan Kim, the successful Smoothie King® franchisee from Korea, bought the Smoothie King® brand from the Kuhnaus. It was a tough decision to sell, but it was the right one. Under Kim's forward thinking leadership, Smoothie King® has expanded domestically and internationally to more than 1,100 locations.

Now almost 50 years later, this organization was blessed to have two *Forward Thinkers* as leaders. When the time was right for the Kuhnaus to move on, the selection of Wan Kim was a great decision to take Smoothie King® to the next level.

To avoid the *Ain't Dere No More* Syndrome, it's important to have the right next generation of *Forward Thinkers* in place to keep the vision fresh.

When you rest on your laurels,
the rest of the world passes you by.
-Jerry LePre

Sing Your Own Song

Sing it Loud. Let Your Voice Be Heard!

Don't be Afraid to Sing.

"You've gotta dance like there's
nobody watching,
Love like you'll never be hurt,
Sing like there's nobody listening,
And live like it's heaven on earth."

- William W. Purkey

7

Let Your Voice Be Heard!

"The human voice is the most perfect instrument of all," Arvo Pärt said.

More and more, the voice of reason is being silenced. In the cancel culture of today, people with common sense are so concerned (afraid) about not being *politically correct,* that their voices of reason refrain from being *honest (genuinely correct).* Thus, they remain silent since *political correctness* often lacks sincerity. Meanwhile, deception, perception, and deflection are tactics used to spin the truth and avoid accountability.

In today's world, it's hard not to offend someone when we speak, especially with social media. After all, there are as many different opinions as there are people. No matter how hard you try, someone will probably be offended by what you say.

Yet silence isn't the solution. Silence never generates effective communication, nor does it enhance relationships. Playing the *politically correct* game by saying things you don't mean isn't the remedy either. It creates hidden agendas, cynicism, resentments, and deeper problems.

Although there's no perfect answer, here are seven *Let Your Voice Be Heard* steps to limit what some may believe to be offensive speech.

Basic Steps to Let Your Voice Be Heard

- Think before you speak. (Most important step.)
- Verify your facts and the credibility of the source.
- Use empathy. When possible, consider the feelings and culture of others.
- Never intentionally offend, condemn, or condescend.
- Stop allowing people to twist the meaning of your words.
- Don't lie, gossip, or spin the truth.
- Choose your words wisely and timely.

Choose Your Words Wisely

Josh took great pride in being the top student in his high school chemistry class. In fact, Josh, who was very conceited, constantly made sure everyone in the school was aware of his scientific brilliance. Like a young Sheldon Cooper[1] of the *Big Bang Theory*, he often interrupted his teacher's lecture to show off his brilliance. His numerous self-centered outbursts were a distraction that often disrupted the classroom.

Thus, it was apparent that Josh's ego was damaged, when Amber, a transfer student, matched Josh's perfect scores on her first three tests. Although Josh's self-image was tainted by Amber's perfection, he often reminded himself he was still number one when it came to vocalizing his knowledge in class. An achievement not shared by his teacher who considered it an attempt to monopolize the classroom.

"How could she do so well on her test, when she never says a word in class," Josh thought. To find the answer, this young Sheldon clone decided to ask Amber that question.

So after the next chemistry period ended, Josh yelled to Amber as she was heading toward the door, "Amber, wait I want to talk to you." But despite Josh's yells, Amber just ignored him and walked off. Josh tried again the next day, but once again, Amber didn't acknowledge him.

Finally, Josh's frustration and anger forced him to confront her during the lunch period. Thus, the self-proclaimed chemistry genius confidently walked across the cafeteria to the table where Amber was sitting with her friends. He coldly looked her in the eye and was about to say something when his chemistry teacher interrupted.

"Is there a problem here?" asked the teacher.

"Yes, there is a real problem here," replied Josh. "Amber refused to acknowledge me when I yelled to her after class. And another thing, how can she get the same grades as me when she never speaks in class?"

The teacher replied, "Amber is deaf. She didn't hear you yelling at her. And if you want to know why she does well in class, I'll tell you. Unlike you, she isn't arrogant. She does not need to speak to express her wisdom. Instead of thinking about how wonderful her voice sounds in class, she is focused on listening and learning what I am teaching. That's right, listening with her eyes by reading my lips."

"Josh, Amber is able to overcome her hearing impairment, but you need to overcome one too," stated the teacher, as Josh looked puzzled at these remarks.

"Josh, your impairment is you speak when it's not appropriate. Everyone knows you are brilliant; you don't have to constantly remind us. I guess you could say, you have a speech impediment," the teacher advised.

Do you have a speech impediment like Josh? We are all guilty of saying things before we have a clear understanding of the facts. Like Josh, we have not always spoken appropriately.

This story taught these lessons regarding choosing your words wisely. Before you say a word, first listen then get all the facts, never speak just to hear your voice, and only speak at the appropriate time. Once done, sing your song as loud and often as you can

Sing it Loud!
Sing Your (Love) Song

"Love is just a word until you find someone to give it meaning," Sharon Meyers (Candance Bergen) from the *Book Club* movie said.

Love is the key to the significance of success. Love opens your heart to identify the passion of your purpose. Once opened, love empowers you to passionately seek what you value most.

Successful *Forward Thinkers* have recognized what they love to do and then did it. They found their purpose and were driven to seek the vision of their destiny.

In fact, this purpose of love is best described as a passion. A passion not only for the vision, but a passion for the journey and the people who you are traveling with and the people who they are traveling for. This is their love song.

The common denominator with successful people from the past and present is they figuratively were not afraid to sing their song of love. They achieved their destiny and fulfilled their purpose with the passion of love.

To discover your key to success, identify what you love and then seek it passionately. Your quest starts with a purpose and comes alive with the love that defines your significance.

Never be afraid to pursue your love song and when the timing is right, sing it as loud as you can.

As I stated before (Fourth Truth), Prof, my guitar teacher, often shared his unique perspective of life and how it related to music. I summarize his viewpoint for singing your love song of life into four statements. *(Expanded version in 'Go the Extra Yard')*

- Don't be afraid to sing your own song;
- Let each note express the passion in your heart and soul;
- Keep singing after you make a mistake; and
- Never stop singing even if no one is listening.

Don't Be Afraid...

Fear is an Illusion

According to comedian Jerry Seinfeld, "Statistics show the number one fear of most people is the fear of speaking in front of a crowd. The number two fear is death. That's right, public speaking is number one and death is number two. This means that for most people attending a funeral, they would rather be in the coffin than give the eulogy."

I admit I have fears. I fear needles. I hate them. I will do anything not to get a shot. I also fear snakes. I fear all types of snakes. I don't discriminate. Poisonous or not, I fear them all.

Let's admit it. We all have fears. Some are small and some are big. But we all have them. What do you fear? What fears are keeping you from popping to the top and staying there?

Keep in mind our fears are preventing us from taking the prudent risks needed for victory. Just like in a horror movie, in most cases fear isn't real. Fear is an illusion that kills the forward-thinking mindset. It creates doubt. Overcoming our fears is necessary if we want to *Pop to the Top*™ and keep our success popping.

To overcome fear, we need four essential attributes depicted by the famous Musketeers of literary and theatrical fame.[2]

The main characters in the historical novels are Porthos, Aramis, and Athos who formed the legendary *Three Musketeers*. They are later joined by young D'Artagnan who comes to Paris to be part of the French soldiers.

Porthos exemplifies the bravery and courage needed to be a risk taker while Athos displays the talent and skill needed to overcome challenges. Aramis provides the wisdom to balance bravery and talent with the passion displayed by D'Artagnan.

Bravery / Porthos

"I learned that courage was not the absence of fear, but the triumph over it. The brave man (person) is not he (she or they) who does not feel afraid, but he (she or they) who conquers that fear," Nelson Mandela said.

Talent / Athos

"Genius is talent set on fire by courage," Henry Van Dyke said. Ignite your passion to consume your fears. Set the world on fire by sharing your talent that was forged by the heat of adversity.

Wisdom / Aramis

"We fear things in proportion to our ignorance of them," Christian Nestell Bovee said. When you know the facts, you conquer fear by being prepared with solutions. You eliminate the element of surprise.

Passion / D'Artagnan

"Passion is energy. Feel the power that comes from focusing on what excites you," Oprah Winfrey said. When fueled by passion, you have the power to conquer fear. You are energized to sing your love song as loud and often as you can.

Know When to Say "NO"

The following is one of my popular signature stories. It offers an impactful message on when and when not to take risks. It's from 'Go the Extra Yard'.

I once had a girlfriend who was trying to kill me. Well, maybe not literally, but she was always coming up with adventurous things for us to do that seemed like she wanted to get me killed. Dinner and a movie weren't enough for her. I don't know for a fact; don't quote me on this, but I think she had a life insurance policy on me.

In her defense, I was a sheltered kid so some things I considered to be daring or risky would be considered fun by most people.

The following is my account of these adventures.

Tubing on the River

The whole thing started with her saying, "Let's go tubing." Despite second thoughts, I decided to go. After all, my girlfriend assured me the water was not deep.

She said, "The river is so shallow that if you have a problem, you can stand up and walk to shore."

She lied!

Since she asked a few friends to go with us, I asked my buddy Bobby, an experienced tuber, to go with us. Thank goodness I did.

The day arrived and we all got into our tubes. There is nothing graceful about getting into a tube.

Consider this: My legs are dangling out at one end of the tube and the top of my body from the waist up is hanging out on the other side. Add to this the fact that my butt is submerged in the river.

Can you get a life size picture of this?

Once situated, we started our journey. I thought tubing was pretty much going with the flow of things. I was wrong.

All the tubers except my friend Bobby and I started using their arms as paddles and were soon out of sight.

Bobby said, "I'll stay with you to make sure you're OK." That's a true friend.

So here we are, slowly going down the river when suddenly, the top of a submerged tree appears in my path. Not a branch but a tree.

I yelled, "Bobby! What should I do?"

Bobby said, "Use your arms to paddle away from it. Be careful. Most of it may be hidden underwater."

I listened to his advice.

A little later, two small water moccasins came swimming toward me. These are poisonous snakes.

I don't like snakes. I really don't like snakes. I thought, "I couldn't get just one, I had to get two."

Once again, Bobby came to my rescue. He told me to use my arms to push water into their path.

"This will force them in a different direction," he said.

After what seemed to me like an eternity, we arrived at our destination. My so-called girlfriend said in a disgusted tone, "What took you so long?"

I told her, "I was just enjoying the ride."

Although I survived, I was left with more than just memories of the trip. I was badly sunburned.

Riding an Old Horse named "Lightning"

My *life-threatening* adventures weren't done. What I believe to be my girlfriend's mission to kill me was now going to part two.

She said, "Let's go horseback riding."

I said, "OK."

When we got to the stables, I told the rancher I hadn't ridden before, so he picked out a very old horse named *Lightning,* who looked like he was ready for the glue factory. I thought, with a name like that, this old boy must have been something special in his day.

The ride began and in a few minutes *Lightning* and I were far behind the rest of the pack. I didn't mind. I was enjoying the scenery.

Then, it started to sprinkle. I thought, "By the time *Lightning* gets me back to the ranch, I will be drenched."

Then, it happened. A flash of lightning appeared in the sky followed by loud thunder. That's when the good old horse named *Lightning* turned into a Triple Crown winner. The old boy bolted off. In a flash, we passed up every other horse and rider ahead of us. *Lightning* was as fast as lightning.

In only a couple of minutes, my horse and I made it back to the stables. We didn't get wet.

What a horse! The old boy still had it. When I arrived, the rancher said, "I guess you now know why he's called *Lightning.*"

Just like my first adventure, I survived. But also like the first, I had not escaped unharmed. My bottom (tush) was badly torn up from going up and down in the saddle.

Skydiving

It was a few weeks later my girlfriend asked, "Let's go skydiving."

That's when I learned to say, "NO!"

10 Lessons for Wisely Taking Risks

Although our journey of life needs to be an adventure, we must make prudent decisions on how, when, and why to take necessary risks. Here are lessons I learned from my adventures.

Four Lessons learned from my tubing adventure:

1. People lie when they want something (the river wasn't shallow);
2. Prepare for unexpected and hidden dangers (submerged tree);
3. Take along an experienced friend (Bobby) to be your guide; and
4. Face trouble head on (water moccasins) to steer it away.

Three Lessons learned from my horseback riding experience:

1. Never judge an ally or a foe by appearance;
2. You may need to find shelter from some storms; and
3. The faster you go, the harder the ride.

Three Lessons learned from NOT skydiving:

1. Take risks to follow your vision not to follow others;
2. Understand your limitations; and
3. Know when to say "NO!"

The biggest risk is not taking any risk.
-Mark Zuckerberg

Conclusion

Step Out from the Crowd

of Conventional Thinkers

"Step out from the crowd.
Boldly GO THE EXTRA YARD™ with the
winners who make a difference. There is no
traffic jam of excuses to block your path to
victory."

- from 'GO THE EXTRA YARD:
Empower the Champion within You'

Stepping Out
It's about Transformation

Forward Thinkers, who step out from the crowd of managers, don't point fingers; they point those who share their journey in the right direction. These innovators lead with vision, values, and purpose while adhering to a high standard of excellence.

As influential communicators, they take the first step to engage, empower, and energize everyone who is part of their journey to the top and above. They connect with respect. To them it's not just about motivation; it's about transformation.

This is your stepping out time to stride in the right direction. Be proactive; not reactive. ***Step Out from the Crowd! Step Up! Stand Out!*** Think forward and GO THE EXTRA YARD to *Stay at the Top*™! (*Recommended reading Go the Extra Yard: Empower the Champion within You / See page 143*)

Stepping Out Advice to Live a Significant Life at the Top

- Stay true to yourself and your core beliefs.
- Never compromise your morals.
- Change to grow; not for the sake of change.
- Don't forget who you are and where you came from.
- Remember those who helped you get to where you are.
- Remain humble and not arrogant.
- Avoid people who want to use you.
- Look beyond the surface to find the truth.
- Standup to bullies.
- Adhere to a high standard of excellence.
- Learn from mistakes and accept the consequences.
- Be happy, life is too short to be otherwise.

We Shouldn't Be So Guarded

When I first started my consulting business many years ago, I did just about everything. I was the receptionist, the janitor, the typist, the check writer, the bill collector, and the CEO. In fact, my company was so small my office was in one of the bedrooms at my home and my office phone was my cell phone. Keep this fact in mind for future reference.

One day, after meeting with a client at his downtown office, I realized my most sought-after prospect, a new property development company, was in the building across the street from my client's office. Since I had some time before my next appointment, I decided to make a cold call. I crossed the street and went into my prospect's building.

I entered the lobby and noticed a security desk with one guard positioned near the elevators. For this story, I am going to refer to this guard as "Barney," since he reminded me so much of Deputy Barney Fife[1], the character on the *Andy Griffith Show*.

I walked up to Barney, stopped, and told him I wanted to meet with the owner of such-and-such company. He asked if I had an appointment.

"No," I said as I handed him my business card.

"Can you please call for me?" I asked.

Barney looked at the card, snorted like the TV character, and said with authority, "It looks legit. This is my first day on the job and you can't be too careful. To make sure, I'll call for you."

Barney rose from his chair and went into the security office located directly behind his desk. I could see everything he was doing since the office had a big picture window.

Barney gave me a suspicious look and turned his back to me. He scrutinized my card as if his life depended on it, picked up the phone, and started to dial.

A few seconds later, my cell phone rang. I took my phone out of my coat pocket and answered the call.

It was Barney.

"Hello," I hesitantly said as I literally began to watch our phone conversation.

Barney boldly said, "Excuse me. I have Mr. Jerry LePre here to see you. Is it OK to send him up?"

Now, I know I asked Barney to make a call for me, but I didn't expect him to make a call to me.

I must apologize, but I got caught up in the moment, so I said, "Great job. You did the right thing to call me. To verify, what does this guy look like?"

Barney turned around, took an intense look at me and said with a no nonsense tone, "He's about six feet tall with dark curly hair. He sort of looks like the guy on *Night Court.*"

I replied, "That's him. Send him up immediately. Also, make sure you validate his parking ticket.

"Yes sir," Barney said. "I was just doing my job."

As soon as Barney hung up the phone, I put my cell phone back into my coat pocket. Barney turned around and walked toward me with a big smile and said, "Sorry about that but I wanted to make sure you were you. Please give me your parking ticket."

In case you were wondering, I didn't want to get Barney in trouble, so I explained to him what happened. We shared a laugh and Barney got me the appointment I wanted.

Life is often like my experience with the security guard. You never know when a great opportunity will appear and who will become your ally. When it comes to forward thinking, we shouldn't be so guarded.

Stay at the Top Motto

On the journey of life,
may you find peace and joy in each moment and
find love and significance that lasts
for an entire lifetime.

Where Do You Go from Here?

In the beginning of this book, I asked this profound question:

Where do you go from here?

The answer is simple but first your perspective of how you define 'At the Top' needs to be examined further.

As mentioned in the introduction, the common meaning of the phrase 'At the Top' refers to a particular identified point. It usually refers to a physical fixed location, like being on the top of a mountain.

Yet your destiny isn't a fixed point.

It's evolving. It's growing.

To the *Forward Thinker*, the phrase 'At the Top' better relates to a treetop. Unlike the highest point on a static mountain, the treetop is alive and growing just as the level of achievement for the *Forward Thinker* is alive and growing to new heights.

For a tree to grow it needs strong roots, a solid trunk, and rain (the water of life). In the same way, *Forward Thinkers* need a strong core of values (trunk) that is rooted in today, showered by discernment, and driven by tomorrow. Also, as the tree grows, it gives life to others by creating seeds. On our climb to the top, we too must plant and cultivate seeds of opportunity that give life to the dreams of others.

So, where do you go from here?

As I said, the answer is simple.

You boldly go where your mind, your heart, and your dreams take you.

You passionately follow your purpose to seek the vision of your destiny.

You step out from the crowd.

You think BIG!

You rise above what life throws your way and make a difference by singing your own song.

Your journey to STAY AT THE TOP starts with one life-changing step. Make sure it's on the path less traveled. The *Seven Significant Truths* of the *Popcorn Principle* are with you every step of the journey.

Don't be insignificant; be significant – Boldly stand out!

Step Forward to Your Destiny.
STAY at the TOP!
Keep climbing to new heights!

Appendix A

12 Life-changing Secrets to Empower Success

(Excerpts from *Smell The Popcorn*)

SECRETS FOR INDIVIDUAL GROWTH

1. Value Your Vision of Who You Are
2. Renew Your Mind with Positive Thoughts
3. Live a Life of Integrity
4. Gain Wisdom from Life's Lessons
5. S.O.A.R. High with Your Goals
   Seek Your Objective and Achieve Your Reward
6. Master Your Moment

SECRETS FOR SHARED GROWTH

7. Love Changes Everything
8. S.P.I.C.E. Up Your Message
   Simplicity, Personality, Imagination, Connection, Entertainment
9. Come Together
10. Give with a Joyful Spirit
11. Serve with Compassion
12. Lead with Vision

Appendix B

V.A.L.U.E. Core

(Excerpts from *Smell The Popcorn*)

Vision

Vision (Purpose) connects our limited consciousness to the unlimited power of possibilities that exist in our imagination. It reveals our purpose, our destination, and our destiny. This insight allows us to envision the end result prior to beginning. Vision stimulates foresight instead of hindsight.

Before we can see where we are going, we must first have a clear vision of who we are, what we seek, who and what we value most, and where we are going. When we have a clear vision, everything else falls into place.

Attitude

Attitude (Perspective) is a state of mind. It can be positive or negative. Either way, this outlook stimulates behavior. Attitude shapes the future. Positive and joyful thoughts generate success while negative thinking creates a paradigm of gloom, doom, and defeat.

Our thoughts, point of view, and disposition determine our perspective on how we live our lives. Will this perspective lead to victory, or will it lead to defeat?

Attitude is a choice. What do you choose?

Love

Love (Passion), when unselfish and unconditional, connects and harmonizes all aspects of our core. Although our quest for significance starts with a clear vision, it is our passion that gives life to our purpose. Passion is the heartbeat of success.

Love's passion should be at the center of our lives and everything we do. Through love we experience joy and value relationships since love defines who and what we value most. Love is the fire of desire.

Understanding

Understanding (Proficiency) empowers our minds, our spirits, our hearts (love), and our bodies. Empowerment originates from the wisdom, proficiency, and prudence gained through the lessons we have learned.

This awareness, which comes from both formal and informal instruction, begins with effective listening and continues with practice. It grows with the passion to build upon past truths, discover new insight, and prepare for the possibilities of tomorrow.

When discernment is applied to our experiences, we transform our dreams into the vision that delineates our significance. We use this awareness to develop and nurture our unique talents and skills that are mental, spiritual, emotional, and physical.

Understanding isn't confined to intellectual and theoretical concepts. It takes action.

Energy

Energy (Power) is the driving force that motivates and strengthens the body, spirit, soul, and mind. It defines consciousness in the physical state. Energy enables us to achieve and maintain the inner strength and physical power that transform dreams into victory. Energy provides the endurance and momentum to perpetuate the joy and rewards of success. While vision is the source, energy is the force. It takes great heat to transform a kernel into popcorn.

"Energy in motion" is a definition of heat.

Appendix C

Are You a Popcorn Person?

(Excerpts from *Smell The Popcorn*)

Definition: A *Popcorn Person*™ is one who, like the kernel of corn, when faced with the heat of adversity, explodes to his (her or they) greatest potential of significance. Unlike a candy bar that melts into a gooey mess and takes the shape of its container, a *Popcorn Person*™ defines and shapes his (her or their) destiny by growing from adversity.

Like a one-of-a-kind snowflake, the *Popcorn* destiny is unique to each individual since there are no two popped kernels and no two *Popcorn Persons* exactly alike.

Are you a *Popcorn Person*™?

Do you *Smell The Popcorn*™ and *Pop to the Top*™?

Are you a **P.O.P.per** (**P**erson **O**f **P**urpose) who is a **TOPPER**?

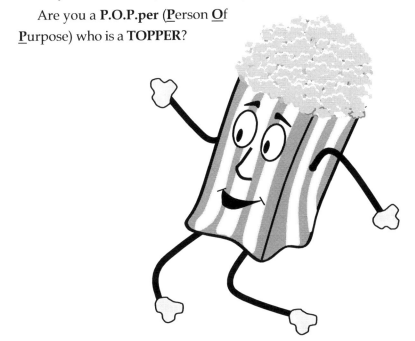

Appendix D

Tactics to Renew Your Mind

(Excerpts from *Smell The Popcorn*)

1. Make the decision to change.

To get something new and positive, you must do something new and positive. Positive change is growth.

Change is a decision to start fresh with the resolve to use a negative catalyst, such as pain, frustration, guilt, loss, or failure, as your reason to make a constructive transformation. Change takes courage. It requires accountability for your words, choices, and actions along with accepting the rewards, responsibilities, and consequences.

2. Be truthful.

Without truth, your vision for change is distorted. Your efforts for renewal will be wasted and you will find yourself in the same rut of uncertainty. When all relationships, actions, and words are based on truth, mental energy and time are never wasted covering up a lie.

3. Make quiet time of meditation a priority.

Meditation is your life-changing time for inspiration and clarification. Once you decide to truthfully change, begin what will become your daily process of meditation. Your initial meditation time determines your purpose and direction of change while your daily meditation refocuses and monitors your path of growth.

4. Maintain a daily journal.

Accountability is important when it comes to monitoring the growth of change. The discoveries learned during your retreat time along with your daily activities should be summarized and written down in your daily journal. This documentation steers you through life's journey by helping you stay on course.

5. Reduce and manage stress.

We live in a fast-paced world filled with deadlines, demands, challenges, and hassles. Technology, which was supposed to reduce pressure, has added to the level of stress.

Although some stress can be motivational, constant stress can be harmful to our body, mind, and overall well-being. It can even stop or slow down our process of change, weaken the immune system, cause headaches, and destroy relationships.

Since stress has become a way of life for most people, it is often difficult or impossible to eliminate. As a result, stress needs to be managed and reduced.

6. Lose emotional baggage.

The emotional baggage from the past, caused by guilt or pain, creates an unnecessary mental burden. It weighs us down and drains our positive energy. This negative mindset prevents the development of new ideas and stops creativity since it forms a blockage caused by anger, frustration, and lack of forgiveness. It can derail our efforts to change.

Forgive those who inflicted the pain and forgive yourself for prior mistakes. Forgiveness transforms negative energy into powerful victories of peace.

7. Eradicate doubt.

Doubt plants the seeds of failure. Doubt creates a false sense of guilt and unnecessary fear that result in a lack of confidence.

A renewed mind eliminates doubt at its roots. In other words, all doubt is eradicated.

8. Balance anger and uncontrolled excitement.

Anger can control the mind while uncontrolled excitement can shift focus onto the moment instead of the vision. Deep-rooted anger and unrestrained excitement are extreme emotions that remove discernment from the thought process.

Although releasing anger and extreme happiness is needed, they cease to be emotions and become the driving force when they are dwelt upon. These excessive mindsets drain the energy from creativity while distorting the paradigm of success.

9. Reflect on the past. (Don't dwell on it. Grow from it.)

We are the sum of our unique experiences. Good, bad, or indifferent, our past decisions and actions make each of us the individuals we are today.

Yet we cannot let our past failures trap us in the old valleys of defeat. Likewise, we cannot allow our prior victories to confine our vision of future greatness. If we choose, we can break free from the past by using the wisdom gained from each challenge and each victory to rise to the next level of success.

10. Anticipate the future.

History records the greatest people of all time were visionaries. They had the gift to anticipate future discoveries or future needs and respond proactively to these opportunities. Anticipation, the skill to envision the future, made them great. Their predictions enabled them to solve or prevent problems before they happen.

Don't waste time in hindsight. Live for today and prepare for tomorrow. Investigate all possibilities.

11. Be accountable to mentors.

Mentors, who serve as guides and act as your conscience, are crucial for renewing your mind. These teachers, leaders, and coaches, who should be of high ethical standing, not only guide you on the right path and keep you focused on your vision, but also hold you accountable for your words and actions.

Mentors serve as role models and help you shape your own unique form of success through correction and direction.

12. Focus mental energy on greatness.

The final tactic for successful change is to focus your mental energy on the greatness inside of you. This empowers your greatness to manifest in your life. Every day focus your mental energy on positive thoughts that forecast success while eliminating negative thoughts that foretell defeat. Your mental outlook shapes the future, so keep your thoughts positive.

Appendix E

Ideal Path for a Conversation

(Excerpts from *Smell The Popcorn*)

A monologue results when one or more parties of a potential conversation aren't serious about speaking or listening. In contrast, an effective dialogue makes great conversation.

An effective dialogue starts when the speaker speaks with S.P.I.C.E. to the listener who listens with empathy, as the following illustration shows.

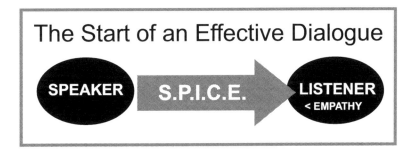

When both speakers converse in this fashion, a conversation develops as soon as both listeners understand the message through empathy and respond accordingly.

This is the ideal path for a conversation as shown below.

On the other hand, a monologue develops when a message sender (not speaker) takes a position of power and control by talking down to the receiver (not listener). This style is based on the sender's wrong perception of the receiver's lower level of comprehension.

Instead of a clear message, the words of a monologue are based on assumptions. This misconception distorts the message shown below.

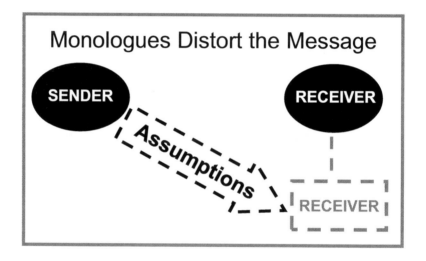

Appendix F

Principles for Building Relationships

(Excerpts from *Smell The Popcorn*)

1. Start with a clean slate.

Don't judge anyone by predetermined prejudices founded on race, gender, age, appearance, finances, etc.

Stop stereotyping. These biases drain energy.

Forgive others and yourself for past mistakes that are repented. Forget old negative thoughts. Don't hold grudges.

Forgive! Forget! Forge ahead!

2. Walk in your partner's shoes.

Before building a meaningful relationship, we must understand the way our partners perceive reality through empathy. In other words, we should take a walk in their shoes. When we see what others see through their eyes, we get a better understanding of our partner's perspective.

This creates vicarious (empathic) insight that enhances perception and response skills. Empathy is a catalyst for effective dialogues that build strong relationships.

3. Get to the truth.

Before we can expect honesty from others, we must be honest with ourselves. This means admitting to our attributes and faults when it comes to building relationships. Being true to a relationship requires a sincere effort to make positive behavior changes when necessary. This forms a bond of trust.

4. Think win-win solutions.

"Think before you speak" is a wise old saying that applies to relationships. Before saying a word to start a conversation, discernment is critical when constructing a message focused on mutual solutions instead of conflict or compromise.

Wisdom empowers win-win solutions that define and refine healthy relationships. It doesn't confine or undermine them.

5. Develop effective dialogues.

Talk is cheap; dialogues are priceless.

Effective dialogues combine empathic listening with zestful messages that instill participation. This is the source of synergy. Great relationships are cultivated with great conversations.

6. Define roles.

Solid relationships grow when all parties maintain a balance of unity while understanding and respecting the rights and multiple roles of each individual. This balance, which creates interdependency, is needed to identify, define, and respect each person's role and position of authority.

Solid relationships are not built on compromise or control. Without interdependency, relationships won't survive since harmonic interaction is a necessity for great partnerships.

7. Clarify expectations.

Associations are destroyed when one party seeks or demands the fulfillment of unrealistic expectations from the others. No one should be expected to give to a relationship what he (she or they) is not capable of giving or doesn't desire to give.

If a person feels expectations can't be met, be honest in the beginning before failure occurs. Honesty measures the strength of the connection while clarifying the parties' commitment to fundamental values, common mission, and vision.

8. Give with prudence and abundance.

Abundant and joyful giving is an extremely important element of successful relationships. It determines the quality and endurance of the connections.

However, we must not foolishly give to people who are using us for our generosity. Give wisely; be prudent.

9. Iron sharpens iron.

A valued friend is free to offer honest constructive criticism, provide a shoulder to lean on, serve as the conscience of accountability, and give wise advice without the fear of jeopardizing the relationship. Close friends encourage, enrich, and inspire. These special partners push each other toward being the best they can be.

10. Make deposits to your emotional bank account.

Relationships grow with deposits to emotional bank accounts. On the other hand, withdrawals can cause relationships to go bankrupt. In our daily interfacing, we choose by our actions and words to make either contributions or extractions.

- **Deposits**
  Here are examples of emotional bank account deposits: clear and defined expectations; courtesy; keeping promises; generosity; kindness; laughter; love; loyalty; smiles; and solutions.
- **Withdrawals**
  Emotional bank account withdrawals include: arrogance; breaking promises; conceit; deceit; discourteous behavior; duplicity; false expectations; lies; manipulation; and pride.

11. Share smiles, laughter, and fun.

A key to a healthy relationship is balancing work with play.

All solid relationships share recreational and social times of fun without losing respect for the other partners. This creates a special bond through laughter. Popcorn always smells better when shared with a friend.

12. Share sorrow and tears.

We all face times of hardships during our lives. No one is immune from loss. The Swedish proverb says it best, "Shared joy is double joy, and shared sorrow is half sorrow."

Notes

Introduction: Stay at the Top™

1. According to Yahoo Answers, no two popped kernels of corn are exactly alike. The only things common are the fundamental particles (atoms) found in the unpopped kernels. When heat causes the kernels to expand, each has a slightly different placement of atoms.
2. *Small Market Radio Newsletter* by Tommy Wyatt and Curtis Lewsey.
3. *8 Traits of a Forward Thinker* by Gilbert Ross.
4. Ibid.
5. Core Values are the ethics and ideals considered in decision making, business practices, relationship building, and problem solving.

Truth #1   Rise and Shine

1. *"Ain't Dere No More"* is a term that is very New Orleans and was made famous by Benny Grunch & The Bunch on their *The Yats of Christmas* album. *"Yat"* is one of my sub-dialects of New Orleans
2. Einstein became a United States citizen in 1940.
3. In 1885, Goode (born a slave) was the first African-American woman to receive a United States patent for a folding bed.
4. Tesla became a United States citizen in 1891.
5. According to PhD Essay, the Constitution is called a *living document*, because like a living changing person, this document can change. Over 240 years ago when this document was written, the framers could never have predicted what changes their future society would have. By leaving phrases unclear it this document is open to interpretation.
6. *8 Traits of a Forward Thinker* by Gilbert Ross.
7. Source: JackieRobinson.com

Truth #2   Think B.I.G.! Think W.O.W.!

1. According to Princeton University, the *Butterfly Effect* is a metaphor that encapsulates the concept of sensitive dependence on initial conditions in chaos theory; namely a small change at one place in a complex system can have large effects elsewhere.
2. *7 Ways to Train Yourself to be a Forward Thinker* by Brad Smith.
3. *How Did Tracy Invented the Smartwatch.* Smithsonian Magazine. The Smithsonian Institution. March 9, 2015.
4. Mark H. McCormack, *What They Don't Teach You at Harvard Business School: Notes from a Street-smart Executive.*
5. Ibid.

Truth #3   Take the Path Less Traveled

1. *What is a Vision Statement?* by Sean Peek.
2. Marshal J. Cook, *10 Minute Guide to Motivating People.*
3. A *Value Statement* lists the ethics and ideals considered in decision making, business practices, relationship building, and problem solving that form your Core Values.
4. *What is a Vision Statement?* by Sean Peek.
5. Ibid.
6. Ibid.
7. *The Essential Elements of a Good Missions Statement* by Lena Eisenstein.

Truth #4   Strike Up the Band

1. *What are the four movements of classical music?* Source: abc.net.au
2. Ibid.
3. Ibid.
4. Ibid.
5. Ibid.
6. Ibid.

7. Reference.com
8. Ibid.
9. For this purpose, organic is defined as happening or developing naturally over time, without being forced.
10. merriam-webster.com/dictionary/diversity
11. merriam-webster.com/dictionary/equity
12. merriam-webster.com/dictionary/inclusive

Truth #5   Make a Difference; Not Excuses

1. Gen. Richard 'Butch' Neal, U.S. Marine Corps (ret) *What Now, Lieutenant?*
2. Ibid.
3. Ibid.
4. Leadership skills I learned from Gen. Neal during my senior year.
5. *Building a Culture of Accountability* from Big Blog posts by the Center for Leadership Studies.
6. Ibid.
7. (a) *How to Create a Culture of Accountability* by Christos Mitsis.

   (b) *Seven Ways to Create a Culture on* Accountability by Jason Richmond, Forbes Councils Member.
8. (a) *What is a Culture of Accountability? (Plus 9 steps to Build It)* by Indeed Editorial Team.

    (b) *7 Keys to Developing a Positive Accountability Culture in Your Organization* by Martin Zwilling.
9. According to Mary Jane Mapes, "An influential leader is someone who, through powerful influence (as opposed to coercion), achieves effective results through people who choose to follow him or her (or them) because they believe in and trust that the leader can guide them to the desired result."
10. (a) *What is a Culture of Accountability? (Plus 9 steps to Build It)* by Indeed Editorial Team.

    (b) *7 Keys to Developing a Positive Accountability Culture in Your Organization* by Martin Zwilling.

11. *Give Yourself Permission to Fail* by Allison Cecile.

12. *Seven Ways to Create a Culture on* Accountability by Jason Richmond, Forbes Councils Member.

13. Ibid.

Truth #6   Avoid the *Ain't Dere No More* Syndrome

1. David Cappello, *The People's Grocer: John Schwegmann, New Orleans, and the Making of the Modern Retail World.*

2. *Makin' groceries* is an old New Orleans term for going to the grocery store. It's a rough translation of the French phrase *faire son marché.*

3. Popeyes.com.sg/ourstory.html

4. ClassicNewYorkHistory.com, *The History of Woolworths.*

5. SmoothieKing.com/our-story

Truth #7   Sing Your Own Song

1. Sheldon Cooper, Ph.D., Sc.D., is a fictional character in the CBS television series *The Big Bang Theory* and its spinoff *Young Sheldon.* Cooper, although a genius, displays a fundamental lack of social skills. *(Source CBS).*

2. The Three Musketeers is a French historical adventure novel written in 1844 by French author Alexandre Dumas.

Conclusion: Step Out from the Crowd

1. Bernard "Barney" Fife is a fictional character in the CBS television series *The Andy Griffith Show.* Fife is a deputy sheriff in the slow-paced, sleepy southern community of Mayberry, North Carolina.

Bibliography

Books:

Brees, Drew. *Coming Back Stronger – Unleashing the Hidden Power of Adversity,* Carol Stream, IL: Tyndale House Publishers, 2010

Chopra, Deepak, Ph.D. *The Seven Spiritual Laws of Success.* San Raphael, CA: Amber Allen Publishing and New World Library, 1994

Cook, Michael J. *10 Minute Guide to Motivating People.* Hoboken, NJ: Macmillan General Reference, 1997

Covey, Stephen R., Ph.D. *The Seven Habits of Highly Effective People.* New York, NY: Simon and Schuster, 1989

Gilliland, Steve. *Making a Difference – A Matter of Purpose, Passion & Pride.* Charleston, SC: Advantage, 2011

Hill, Napoleon. *Think and Grow Rich.* Meriden, CT: The Ralston Society, 1938

Kelley, Rhonda Harrington, Ph.D. *Divine Discipline – How to Develop and Maintain Self-Control.* Gretna, LA: Pelican Publishing Company, 1992

MacArthur, John. *The Book on Leadership.* Wolgemuth and Associates, 2004

Maxwell, John C. *Leadership Promises for Every Day.* Nashville, TN: J. Countryman, 2003

Maxwell, John C. *The Power of Thinking Big.* Tulsa, OK: River Oak Publishing, 2001

Neal, Richard, Gen. *What Now, Lieutenant?* Jacksonville, FL: Fortis, 2019

Peale, Norman Vincent, Ph.D. *The Amazing Results of Positive Thinking*. New York, NY: Fireside, 2003 (reprint)

Peale, Norman Vincent, Ph.D. *The Power of Positive Thinking*. New York, NY: Simon and Schuster, 2005 (reprint)

Peale, Norman Vincent, Ph.D. *Stay Alive All Your Life*. New York, NY: Fireside, 2003 (reprint)

Peck, M. Scott, MD. *The Road Less Traveled*. New York, NY: Simon and Shuster, 1985

Smallwood, Beverly, Ph.D. *This Wasn't Supposed to Happen to Me*. Nashville, TN: Thomas Nelson, 2007

Warren, Rick, Ph.D. *The Purpose Driven Life*. Grand Rapids, MI: Zondervan, 2002

Audio Books:

Covey, Stephen R., Ph.D. *Living the 7 Habits*. Provo, UT: Covey Leadership Center

Covey, Stephen R., Ph.D. *Principle-Centered Leadership*. Provo, UT: Covey Leadership Center

MacArthur, John. *Characteristics of an Effective Leader*. Grace to You, 1998

Robbins, Anthony. *Awake the Giant Within*, New York, NY: Simon and Schuster, 1991

Ziglar, Zig. *Goals : Setting and Achieving Them on Schedule*. Chicago, IL: Nightingale-Conant Audio, 1988

About the Author

Jerry LePre is a highly effective speaker, award-winning journalist (LPA), trainer, and author who engages and energizes business, civic, and educational organizations to *Empower the Champion Within*. His result-oriented books, messages, and presentations blend practical insight and old-fashioned values with humor, common sense, and uplifting stories.

For more than two decades, the thought-provoking teaching resources created by this New Orleans native have been used for talent, culture, and leadership development by Ochsner, Fortune 100 companies, United States Coast Guard (USCG), Jefferson Parish Chamber of Commerce, and Bethany Church (Lazarus Program). Jerry taught educators in Orleans Parish, Jefferson Parish, St. Bernard Parish, and St. John Parish.

Jerry's motivational books, keynotes, consultations, and training programs are designed to empower you to change, grow, and learn by using the heat of adversities as the catalyst to achieve significance.

His multi-media sessions feature bold graphics, heart-warming stories, humor, influential passion, and practical solutions. His engaging programs inspire and energize productivity while defining your purpose, perspective, passion, prudence, and power.

The empowering work of this renaissance man isn't just about motivation, it's focused on transformation.

Jerry is the founder of Celebrate Senior Life (CSL) that provides informative, engaging, and entertaining presentations to empower senior adults. He's an award-winning classical guitarist, singer, and songwriter along with being a digital graphic artist. He is the creator of the *Blue Seagull* style of art.

Professional Highlights

- Co-hosted WYES's *Pulse New Orleans*
- Featured columnist for *GriulWeek*
- Two books ranked in the top 110 by Amazon*
- *Who's Who* New Orleans Honoree
- Board member *National Speakers Association* (NSA) GNO**
- Director of Ochsner Health Plan's *Total Health 65*
- International Risk Manager for Non-profit
- Chief Negotiator National Accounts / Non-profit
- Member of the *Southern Christian Writers Guild* (SCWG)
- *Key to the City* of New Orleans for academic excellence
- Featured on TV and Radio *(Family Focus / LifeSongs)*
- Award-winning Journalist (LPA)
- Blogger: Senior Sense
- Guest Blogger for Customer Service Guru Shep Hyken

*Two books rated in top 110 for Christian Stewardship / July 2021
** Regional board member 2016-17

Some of Jerry's other books (available on Amazon) include:

- ✓ *Smell The Popcorn – 12 Life-changing Secrets to Pop to the Top,* Joyful Life Publishing, 2018 (second edition/ See next page);
- ✓ *Go the Extra Yard – Empower the Champion within You,* Joyful Life Publishing, 2018 (Standard second edition/ See next page);
- ✓ *ChristianNOMICS: God's Master Plan for Financial Freedom,* Joyful Life Publishing, 2020; 2021 (See page 144); and
- ✓ *Above the Water Line - Words and Art to Inspire the Soul:* Joyful Life Publishing; 2019.

JerryLePre.com
CelebrateSeniorLife.com

Featured Inspirational Books by Jerry LePre

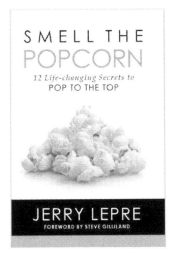

Smell the Popcorn
12 Life-changing Secrets to
Pop to the Top

Popcorn starts with a tiny kernel that expands when faced with extreme heat. In the same way, we can seize our opportunities of success by being transformed by the heat of adversity. Through insightful stories, humor, graphs, and practical wisdom, this book provides proven and easy-to-implement strategies to *Pop to the Top*™ through 12 life-changing secrets. *(Available in a faith-based edition.)*

Go the Extra Yard
Empower the champion within you

If you are falling short of your destiny, focus on your goal and not on the fear of taking your next step to victory. In this engaging and empowering book, Jerry LePre energizes his readers to *Go the Extra Yard*™ with seven keys to victory for the game of life. Through heart-warming stories, practical insight, humor, and common sense, this book provides what it takes to *Go the Extra Yard. (Available in a faith-based edition.) Companion 30-day devotional: Be the Champion You are Meant to Be.*

ChristianNOMICS

God's Master Plan for Financial Freedom

Practical and Spiritual Wisdom to Build a Life of Joy and Prosperity

(Rated by Amazon as High as 110 for Christian Stewardship Books in July of 2021)

In these uncertain economic times, although our politicians don't have the answer on how to fix this crisis, the Word of God offers the solution. Stewardship expert Jerry LePre teaches faith-based practical wisdom to discover peace, joy, and independence.

In addition to learning 17 essential principles for living financially free, this book provides over 100 tactics to stretch and conserve your hard-earned dollars. Jerry's easy-to-implement SEVEN BUILDING BLOCK STRATEGIES, which start with a Christ-centered financial freedom plan (budget), create, increase, manage, and protect your finances. *(Available in a senior adult edition.)*

Explore these life-changing topics to overcome inflation.

- Pay less at the pump
- Save money at the grocery store
- Lower insurance costs
- Techniques to reduce federal taxes
- How to establish good credit
- Use God's four primary purposes for money
- AND MUCH MORE!

Companion Workbook: Champion Stewards Guide to Empower a Debt-Free Lifestyle.

Joyful Life Publishing

JerryLePre.com
JoyfulLifePublishing.com
CelebrateSeniorLife.com

Joyful Life Publishing (JLP) provides professional, quality, and cost-effective self-publishing options for authors.

JLP utilizes our customized concepts that offer flexibility of choice from an À LA CARTE portfolio of valuable _concierge_ services. Our process allows authors to keep total _control_ of their projects with a broad scope of global _circulation_ options.

The JLP team energizes, encourages, and supports writers through every step of the self-publishing process.

Do you have a powerful story to tell?

If so, now is the time to tell it in your book. Your words make a difference. Be a difference maker.

SHARE YOUR JOY! GET THE 'WRITE' ATTITUDE!

Made in the USA
Columbia, SC
26 February 2024

32012786R00080